CW00542278

DISCOVERING TUTANKHAMUN

Paul Collins

Liam McNamara

Discovering Tutankhamun

24 July–2 November 2014

Copyright ©Ashmolean Museum,
University of Oxford, 2014

Paul Collins and Liam McNamara have
asserted their moral rights to be identified
as the authors of this work.

British Library Cataloguing in Publications Data

A catalogue record for this book is
available from the British Library

EAN 13: 978 1 85444 287 1

All rights reserved. No part of this publication may be
transmitted in any form or by any means, electronic
or mechanical, including photocopy, recording
or any storage and retrieval system, without the
prior permission in writing of the publisher.

Book designed by Vermillion

Printed and bound in Malta by Gutenberg Press

For further details of Ashmolean titles please visit:
www.ashmolean.org/shop

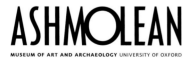

MUSEUM OF ART AND ARCHAEOLOGY UNIVERSITY OF OXFORD

Image credits

All images ©The Griffith Institute, University of
Oxford, with the following exceptions: ©Ashmolean
Museum, University of Oxford p.14, 15 (right), 45
(bottom), 52–53, 91, 93; ©Birmingham City Library
(Benjamin Stone Archive) p.16; ©Bridgeman Art
Library p.90; ©Brier-Remler Collection p.68–69, 70,
76 (bottom); ©British Airways p.86 (top); ©Trustees
of the British Museum p.15 (left), 95; ©Corbis
Images p.6–7; ©Factum Arte p.96; ©Highclere Castle
p.19 (left); ©Kenneth Garrett p.12; ©Metropolitan
Museum of Art, New York p.18, 23, 88, 94;
©Museum of London p.72 (left); Private Collections
p.19 (right), 62, 64, 67, 71, 73 (top), 74, 76 (top),
80, 81, 85, 86 (bottom), 101 (bottom); ©Royal
Botanic Gardens, Kew p.54; ©Semmel Concerts
p.98–99; ©The Illustrated London News p.75,
78–79; ©The Times Newspapers p.63; ©University
of Liverpool p.87; ©Victoria and Albert Museum,
London p.72 (centre), 73 (right) and inside covers.

Front: Glass plate negative made at the time of
excavation, showing the face of Tutankhamun's
outermost gilded coffin, illuminated on a 1930s light box.

Back: Photograph by Harry Burton of the intact rope
and mud sealing on the gilded shrines enclosing
Tutankhamun's sarcophagus.

Inside covers: Chiffon decorated with gilt threads and
printed squares, about 1925.

Generously supported by The Selz Foundation
Media Partner: The Times
Additional support from Savills

Contents

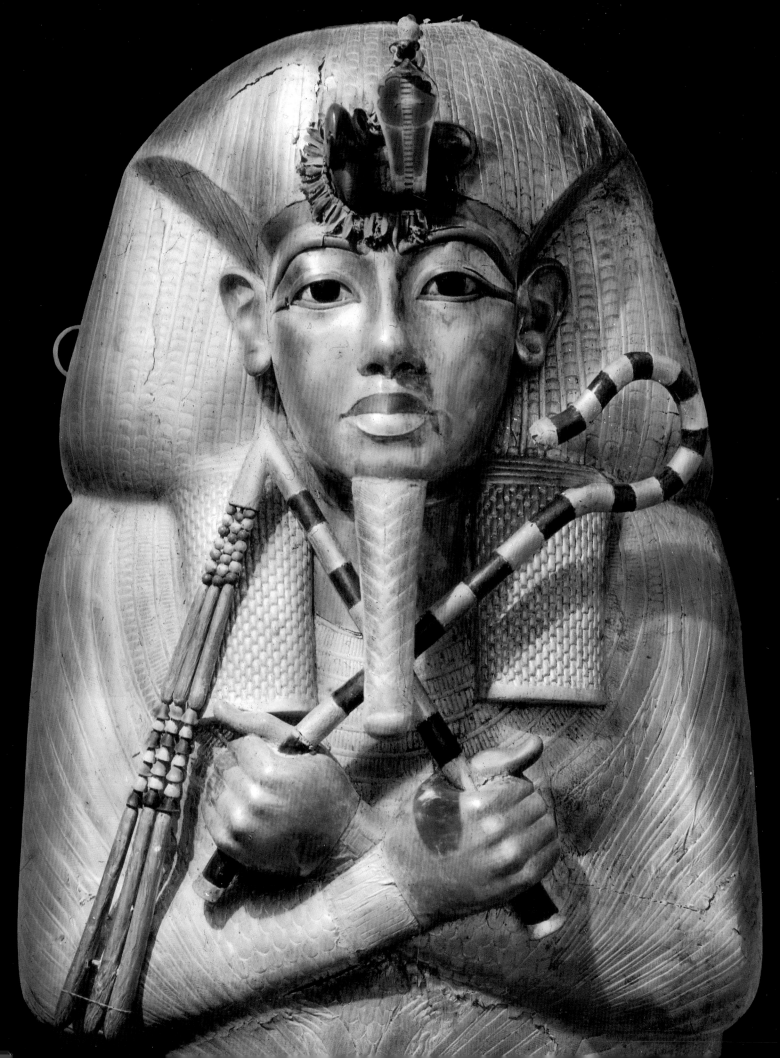

Foreword

The year 2014 marks the 75th anniversary of the founding of the University of Oxford's Griffith Institute. The Institute was established by Francis Llewellyn Griffith, Oxford's first Professor of Egyptology, who left a substantial part of his estate for the creation of 'a permanent home or institute for the study of the ancient languages and antiquities of the Near East … in or adjacent to, the Ashmolean Museum'. The association between the Museum and the Institute – one the home to a world renowned collection of artefacts from ancient Egypt, Sudan and the Near East, the other the repository of an archive of some of Egyptology's greatest scholars, and each centres of scholarly research – has been maintained both physically and intellectually ever since. It seemed appropriate therefore to celebrate this long relationship by exhibiting some of the Institute's greatest treasures to tell the story of Lord Carnarvon and Howard Carter's remarkable discovery of the tomb of Tutankhamun in Egypt's Valley of the Kings in 1922.

The Ashmolean is of course a museum of both art and archaeology, and they are brought together in this exhibition. Howard Carter was a meticulous archaeologist who would take an astonishing ten years to record the contents of Tutankhamun's tomb. He was also a talented artist and draughtsman who, along with other contemporary artists, captured in pencil drawings and paintings the detail and vibrancy of many of the objects he uncovered. Of equal importance was the archaeological photography of Harry Burton, who produced images that are works of art in their own right. The exhibition also explores the impact of the discovery on the fashion and politics of the 'Roaring Twenties,' and investigates what the tomb's contents can tell us about Tutankhamun and his time though spectacular ancient objects drawn from the Ashmolean's own collections as well as major international loans.

People in many countries have contributed to this enterprise, and they are mentioned in the acknowledgments by the exhibition curators Paul Collins and Liam McNamara on page 104. An undertaking of this scope cannot be presented without major financial support. The Museum extends its sincere gratitude to the Selz Foundation for their exceptional generosity toward this project. In addition, we are grateful to Savills for their important contribution.

Professor Christopher Brown CBE
Director

◐ Howard Carter's hand-tinted glass lantern slide showing Tutankhamun's outermost coffin.

◑ The Fifth Earl of Carnarvon (second from left) and his daughter, Lady Evelyn Herbert, arriving at Luxor railway station on 18 February 1923, are met by the local Egyptian governor (right).

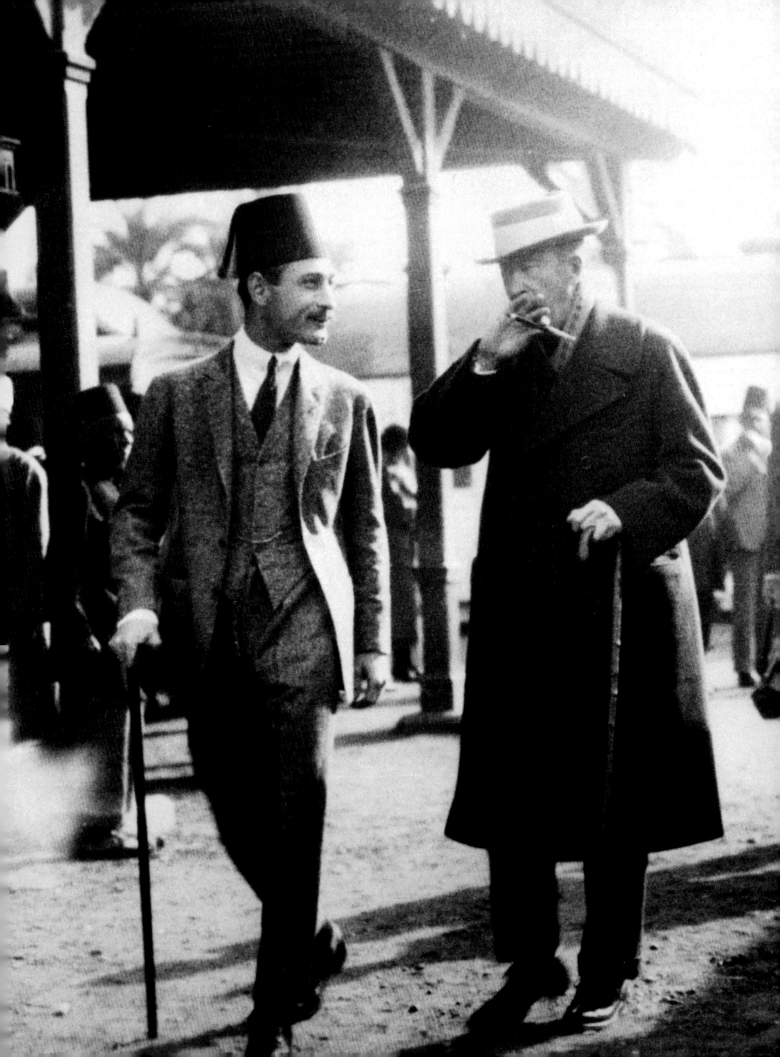

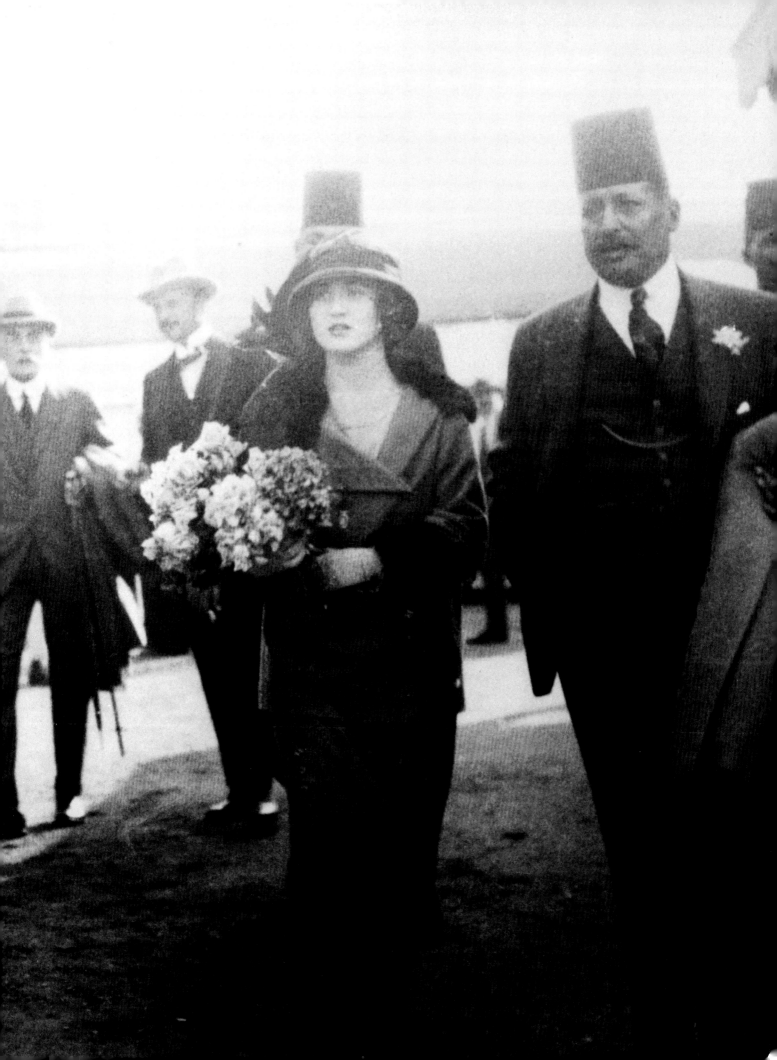

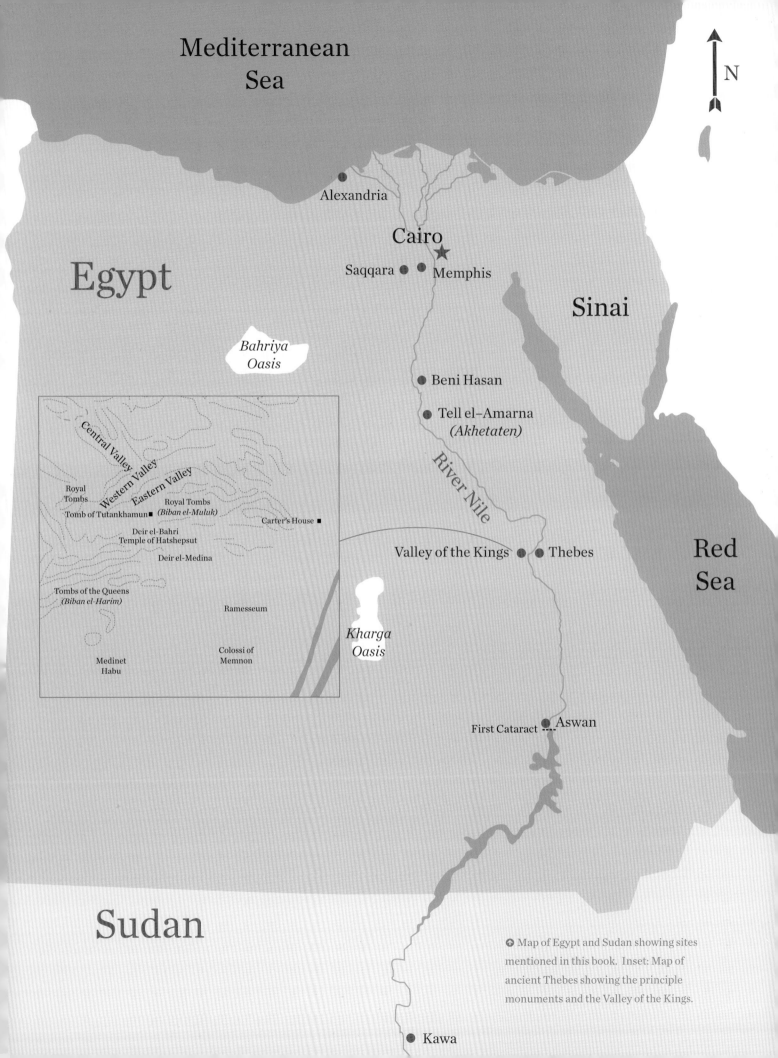

Mediterranean
Sea

Egypt

Sinai

Alexandria

Cairo

Saqqara • • Memphis

Bahriya
Oasis

Beni Hasan

Tell el–Amarna
(Akhetaten)

River Nile

Central Valley

Western Valley

Eastern Valley

Royal
Tombs

Royal Tombs
(Biban el-Muluk)

Tomb of Tutankhamun ■

Carter's House ■

Deir el-Bahri
Temple of Hatshepsut

Deir el-Medina

Tombs of the Queens
(Biban el-Harim)

Ramesseum

Kharga
Oasis

Valley of the Kings • • Thebes

Red
Sea

Medinet
Habu

Colossi of
Memnon

First Cataract ---- • Aswan

Sudan

⬆ Map of Egypt and Sudan showing sites
mentioned in this book. Inset: Map of
ancient Thebes showing the principle
monuments and the Valley of the Kings.

Kawa

N

Chronology of Ancient Egypt

All dates before 664 BC are approximate.

Predynastic (prehistoric) Period 5300–3100 BC

'Dynasty 0' 3300–3100 BC

Early Dynastic Period 3100–2575 BC

1st Dynasty 3100–2890 BC

2nd Dynasty 2890–2686 BC

3rd Dynasty 2686–2575 BC

Old Kingdom 2575–2125 BC

4th Dynasty 2575–2450 BC

5th Dynasty 2450–2325 BC

6th Dynasty 2325–2175 BC

7th and 8th Dynasties 2175–2125 BC

First Intermediate Period 2125–1975 BC

9th, 10th (northern) and 11th (southern) Dynasties 2125–1975 BC

Middle Kingdom 1975–1640 BC

11th Dynasty (after reunification) 1975–1940 BC

12th Dynasty 1940–1755 BC

13th and 14th Dynasties 1755–1640 BC

Second Intermediate Period 1640–1540 BC

15th and 16th Dynasties (Lower Egypt) 1640–1540 BC

17th Dynasty (Upper Egypt) 1640–1540 BC

New Kingdom 1540–1075 BC

18th Dynasty 1540–1292 BC

Ahmose 1540–1514 BC

Amenhotep I 1514–1493 BC

Thutmose I 1493–(?) BC

Thutmose II (?)–1479 BC

Thutmose III 1479–1425 BC

Hatshepsut 1473–1458 BC

Amenhotep II 1426–1400 BC

Thutmose IV 1400–1390 BC

Amenhotep III 1390–1353 BC

Amenhotep IV/Akhenaten 1353–1335 BC

Smenkhkare 1335–1332 BC

Tutankhamun 1332–1322 BC

Ay 1322–1319 BC

Horemheb 1319–1292 BC

19th Dynasty 1292–1190 BC

20th Dynasty 1190–1075 BC

Third Intermediate Period 1075–715 BC

21st Dynasty 1075–945 BC

22nd Dynasty 945–715 BC

23rd Dynasty 830–715 BC

24th Dynasty (Sais) 730–715 BC

25th Dynasty (Nubia and Theban area) 770–715 BC

Late Period 715–332 BC

25th Dynasty (Nubia and all Egypt) 715–657 bc

26th Dynasty 664–525 BC

27th Dynasty (Persian) 525–404 BC

28th Dynasty 404–399 BC

29th Dynasty 399–380 BC

30th Dynasty 380–343 BC

'31st Dynasty' (2nd Persian Period) 343–332 BC

Greek, Roman and Byzantine Periods 332 BC–AD 641

Macedonian Dynasty 332–305 BC

Ptolemaic Dynasty 305–30 BC

Roman and Byzantine emperors 30 BC–AD 641

Arab domination AD 639–641

Based on John Baines and Jaromir Malek, *Cultural Atlas of Ancient Egypt* (New York: Checkmark Books, 2000) and Helen Whitehouse, *Ancient Egypt and Nubia in the Ashmolean Museum* (Oxford: Ashmolean Museum, 2009).

The Griffith Institute

'A permanent home or institute for the study of the ancient languages and antiquities of the Near East ... in or adjacent to, the Ashmolean Museum.'

In 2014 the Griffith Institute celebrated its 75th anniversary. As the centre for a number of major research projects, the Institute lies at the heart of Egyptology and Ancient Near Eastern Studies within the University of Oxford. It is also home to an archive of some of Egyptology's greatest scholars, including those of its founder Francis Llewellyn Griffith, the first Professor of Egyptology at Oxford, and Sir Alan Gardiner, the pre-eminent scholar of ancient Egyptian language. However, the most famous records in its care are surely those of British archaeologist Howard Carter, the discoverer of the tomb of Tutankhamun.

Carter bequeathed the archive to his niece, Phyllis Walker, who generously presented it to the University of Oxford shortly after the archaeologist's death in 1939. The records, which document the excavation of Tutankhamun's tomb in extraordinary detail, consist of approximately 3,150 record cards and some 1,850 black and white glass negatives taken by the excavation's photographer, Harry Burton. There are also Carter's pocket diaries, journals and excavation plans, as well as conservation records for individual objects and thousands of pages of notes made in preparation for the final publication of the tomb and its contents. Between 1995 and 2012 the entire archive was digitised and made fully available on the Griffith Institute's website: *www.griffith.ox.ac.uk*

Howard Carter's excavation of Tutankhamun's tomb was one of the most significant archaeological discoveries of the twentieth century. The name of Egypt's 'boy king' is now synonymous with the glories of ancient Egyptian civilisation, and the spectacular contents of his tomb continue to capture the public's imagination. Millions of people have visited his tomb in the Valley of the Kings and seen the objects on display

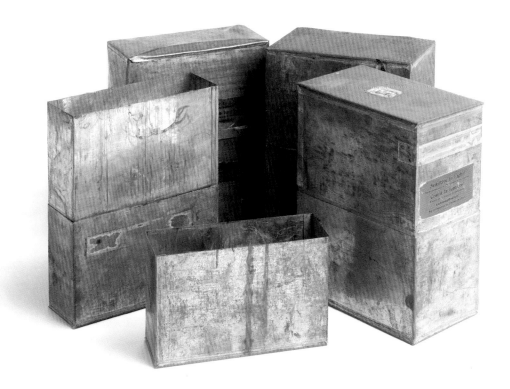

⊘ Metal canisters for holding the light sensitive glass plates used by Harry Burton, the excavation's photographer.

in the Egyptian Museum in Cairo. Millions more have viewed selected items that have travelled the globe in major exhibitions, read countless books and watched television documentaries devoted to the pharaoh.

It may therefore come as something of a surprise to learn that the majority of the objects from Tutankhamun's tomb have not yet been fully studied. The recording of the tomb, and the removal and packing of its contents for transfer to Cairo, took Howard Carter and his team an astonishing 10 years. Carter intended to publish a definitive report of the discovery, based upon his extensive notes, but this was curtailed by strained relations with his Egyptological colleagues and an illness that cut his career short: Carter died just seven years after he had completed work in the tomb, having published a three-volume preliminary report, *The Tomb of Tut. Ankh.Amen*. Subsequently the exceptional character of the discovery, with its large proportion of gold items requiring high levels of security, and the need for specialised knowledge beyond Egyptology on the part of researchers have significantly slowed progress. To date only some 30 per cent of the material has been the subject of detailed scholarly study and publication. There remains, therefore, enormous potential for the Carter Archive to illuminate the world of Tutankhamun.

This book draws on the records in the Griffith Institute to show how they remain fundamental for telling the story of Tutankhamun. Equally significant, however, is the role that the archive plays in the on-going work of researching and preserving the tomb and its contents. It is hoped that the material presented here will inspire the next generation of scholars and students to continue the work of discovering Tutankhamun.

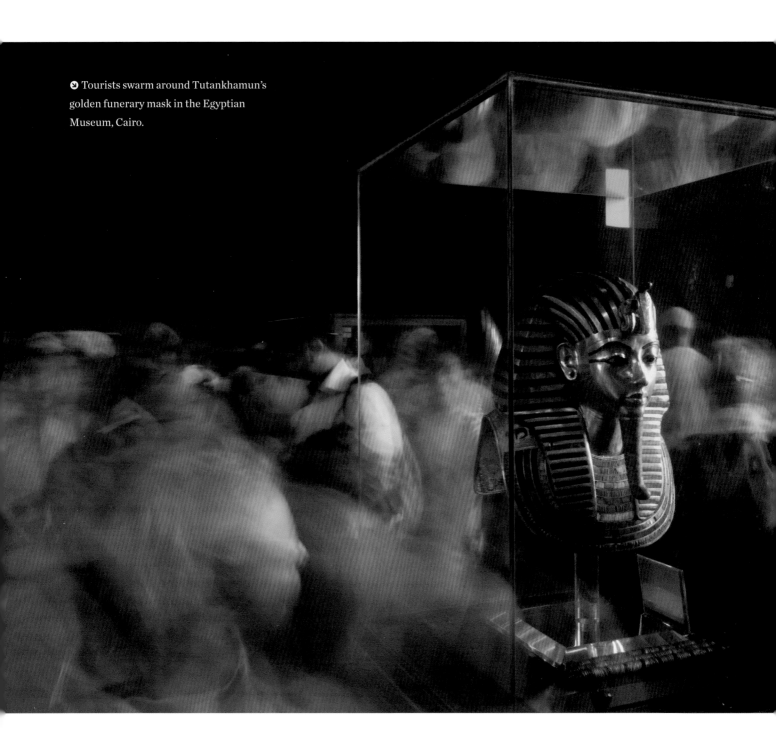

◗ Tourists swarm around Tutankhamun's golden funerary mask in the Egyptian Museum, Cairo.

Tutankhamun before 1922

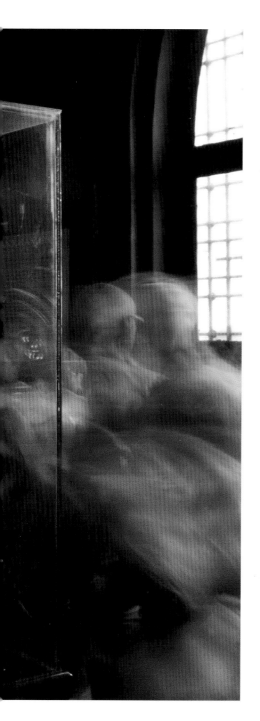

It is probably no exaggeration to say that the discovery of Tutankhamun's tomb is firmly established in the world's collective consciousness, permeating both high and low culture. The pharaoh's golden funerary mask is arguably one of the most recognisable icons of the modern world. Indeed, the Tutankhamun 'phenomenon' has now flourished for nearly a century and shows little sign of abating. However, in the years immediately prior to the discovery of the king's tomb in 1922, the name of Tutankhamun was known only to a few specialists.

The decipherment of Egyptian hieroglyphs in the 1820s made it possible to reconstruct Egypt's ancient history independent of the records of Greek and Roman authors. Tutankhamun's name as inscribed on a number of surviving monuments and objects could now be read, but he appeared to be a minor, perhaps illegitimate king overshadowed by more illustrious monarchs. Indeed, his name was missing from ancient lists of rulers that were intended to demonstrate the unbroken nature of Egyptian kingship across thousands of years. This immense span of time had been divided since antiquity into 30 or 31 dynasties of kings, grouped by modern scholars into periods of political unity, so-called 'Kingdoms', separated by periods of fragmentation called 'Intermediate Periods' (see Chronology, p. 9). Other hieroglyphic sources, however, placed Tutankhamun among the last rulers of the 18th Dynasty (about 1540–1292 BC), a period that witnessed the establishment of a vast Egyptian empire and royal building projects on a colossal scale, including the great temple complexes at Thebes (modern Karnak and Luxor).

The history of the late 18th dynasty became better known after 1887, when a cache of over 300 inscribed clay tablets was discovered at the site of Tell el-Amarna in Middle Egypt. These 'Amarna letters' record the international correspondence between the rulers of the Near East and the Egyptian kings Amenhotep III (about 1390–1353 BC), Amenhotep IV (about 1353–1335 BC), and possibly Tutankhamun (about 1332–1322 BC). Encouraged by the find, the British archaeologist William Matthew Flinders Petrie undertook excavations at Tell el-Amarna in 1891–92. This was followed by extensive work by German archaeologists from 1907 to 1914 which resulted in significant discoveries, including the recovery of the famous painted bust of Queen Nefertiti.

It became apparent that the site of Tell el-Amarna (ancient Akhetaten, 'the Horizon of the Aten') had been established on virgin soil by the King Amenhotep IV as a royal and sacred settlement. As work on his city began, around the sixth year of the king's reign, Amenhotep changed his name to Akhenaten (which may be translated as 'He who is beneficial to the Aten'). He abandoned the cult of the traditional state gods, especially the god Amun of Thebes, to focus devotion on a single deity, the disc of the sun called the 'Aten'. Akhenaten and his wife Nefertiti presented themselves as the intermediaries between their human subjects and the Aten, and were accordingly worshipped in their own right. When Akhenaten died he was succeeded briefly by the mysterious individual Smenkhkare (about 1335–1332 BC), before Tutankhaten ('Living image of the Aten') came to the throne.

The extraordinary character of Akhenaten was discussed in both scholarly and popular literature throughout the late nineteenth and early twentieth centuries. When, for example, the Egyptologist James Henry Breasted published in 1916 a best-selling textbook, *Ancient Times: A History of the Early World*, he devoted over two pages to this king, presenting him as a visionary and an idealist who attempted, but ultimately failed, to introduce monotheism. Tutankhaten, who reversed the Aten revolution, returned the religious capital to its traditional centre at Thebes and adopted the name Tutankhamun ('Living image of Amun'), receives no mention in Breasted's account.

⊙ Detail from a fragmentary wall painting excavated at Tell el-Amarna depicting two of the six daughters of King Akhenaten and Queen Nefertiti, about 1345–1335 BC.

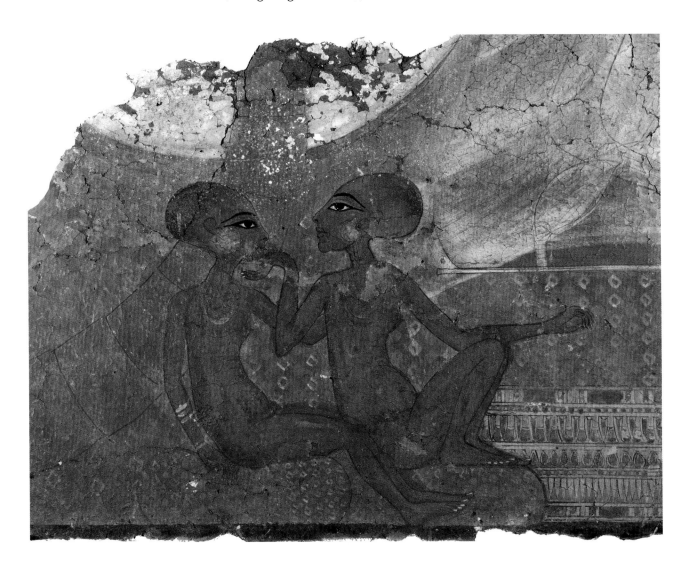

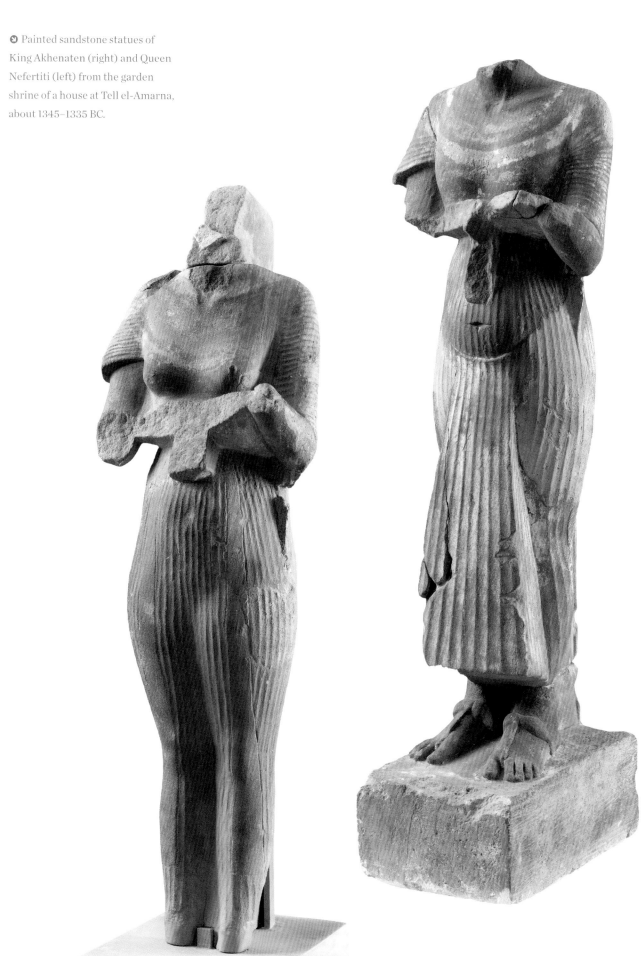

Painted sandstone statues of King Akhenaten (right) and Queen Nefertiti (left) from the garden shrine of a house at Tell el-Amarna, about 1345–1335 BC.

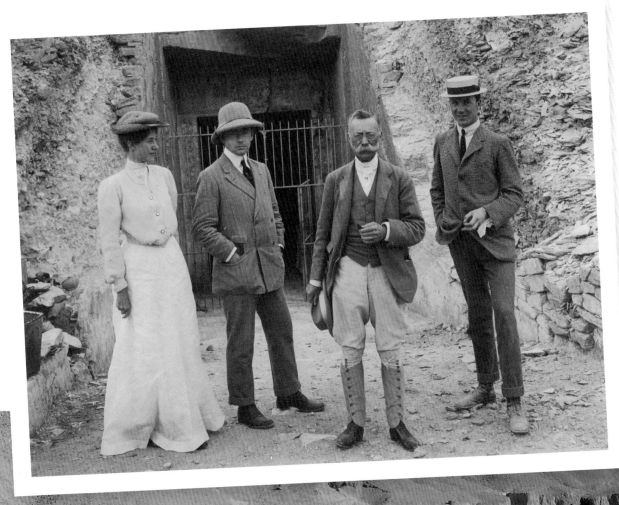
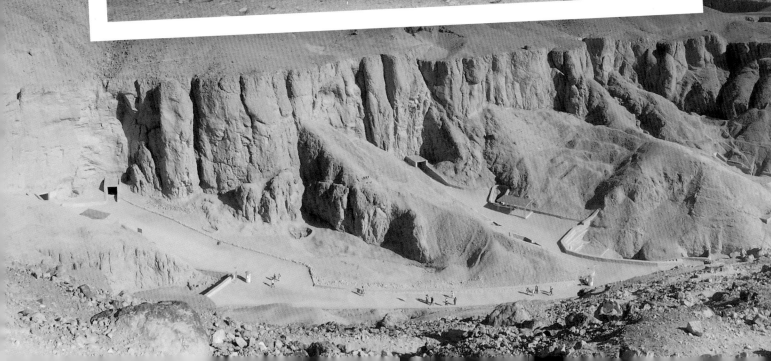

The Search for Tutankhamun

The Valley of the Kings

The Valley of the Kings lies on the west bank of the River Nile, opposite the ancient city and temples of Thebes (modern Luxor) in the south of Egypt. Formed over millennia from seasonal flood waters that cut a ravine through the limestone cliffs, the Valley consists of east and west branches. It was the eastern valley that was chosen as the burial place for nearly every ruler of the so-called New Kingdom (about 1540–1075 BC). The vast majority of these royal tombs were plundered in antiquity; by the Roman period some were already attracting tourists, as evidenced by the presence of Greek and Roman graffiti. In 1799 members of Napoleon Bonaparte's Expedition to Egypt drew maps and plans of the known tombs, and throughout the nineteenth century many more were discovered or cleared. One of the most intensive periods of work in the Valley was undertaken between 1902 and 1914 under the sponsorship of Theodore Montgomery Davis, a wealthy, retired New York lawyer and amateur archaeologist. Davis was granted the concession to excavate the Valley of the Kings by the Egyptian Antiquities Service, and employed his own archaeologist to conduct the work; from 1905–1908 this was a young Englishman, Edward Russell Ayrton.

◐ Theodore Davis flanked by archaeologist Edward Ayrton (right) and the Inspector-General of Antiquities for Upper Egypt, Arthur Weigall, and his wife Hortense (left), 1907.

◑ Panoramic view across the Valley of the Kings.

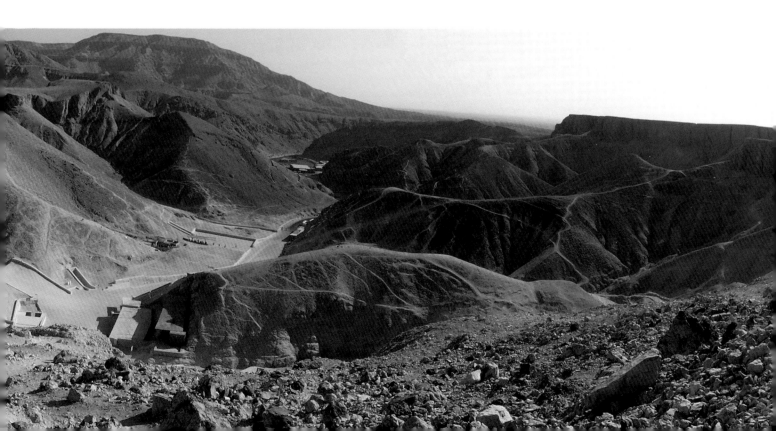

Important Clues

In the winter of 1907 Ayrton discovered a small pit (approximately 2 by 1.25 metres, and 1.4 metres at its deepest point) cut into the bedrock of the Valley. Packed into this space was a collection of large pottery jars which had been filled with pieces of linen, broken mud seals, sacks containing natron (a salt used in the mummification process) and sawdust, collars of faded flowers, and a great number of broken pots. There were also animal bones and vessel covers made from reeds. Theodore Davis donated this apparently meaningless collection to the Metropolitan Museum of Art in New York. The objects were recognised by Herbert Winlock, curator of the museum's Egyptian Department, as materials used by ancient Egyptian embalmers, as well as the remnants of a banquet held at the time of a funeral. Significantly, the name written on some of the mud seals and torn linen was that of Tutankhamun.

Two years after Ayrton's discovery, in 1909, the tomb of Tutankhamun was discovered. At least that is what Davis believed. The alleged tomb was a small, undecorated, underground chamber filled with dried mud, in which was found an un-inscribed alabaster funerary figure (*shabti*) and a broken wooden box with pieces of gold leaf embossed with the names of Tutankhamun, Ankhesenamun (Tutankhamun's wife), and Ay (Tutankhamun's vizier and successor).

While these fragmentary finds suggested that Tutankhamun's tomb might indeed lie somewhere in the Valley of the Kings, many Egyptologists recognised that the actual burial had yet to be discovered. Theodore Davis, however, believed that there was nothing left to uncover, and in the introduction to his 1912 publication, *The Tombs of Harmhabi and Touatânkhamanou*, he wrote: 'I fear that the Valley of the Tombs is now exhausted'. Two years later he gave up his concession to excavate.

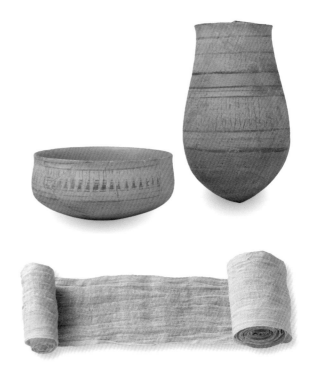

⊘ Linen bandage and pottery vessels from so-called Pit 54 discovered by Edward Ayrton in 1907.

Lord Carnarvon and Howard Carter

When Theodore Davis gave up his right to excavate in the Valley of the Kings in 1914, the concession was acquired by an English aristocrat, George Edward Stanhope Molyneux Herbert, Fifth Earl of Carnarvon.

Herbert had succeeded his father to the earldom in 1890, at the age of 24; he had already travelled extensively, including to Egypt, and was extremely well-read. Five years later he married Almina Wombwell, daughter of the banker Alfred de Rothschild. Aided by Almina's considerable wealth, Carnarvon was able to indulge his passions for racehorses and fast cars. It was a serious motoring accident in 1901 that led Lord Carnarvon to Egyptology; badly injured, he decided to spend the winter months convalescing in the warm climate of Egypt where he developed an interest in archaeological excavation. Like Theodore Davis,

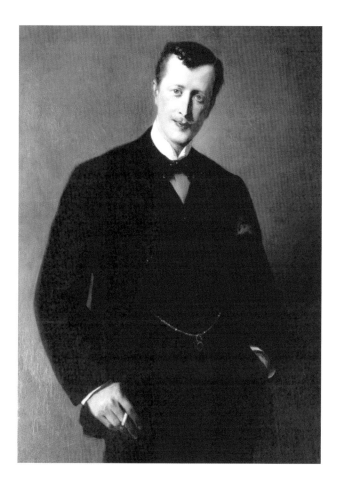

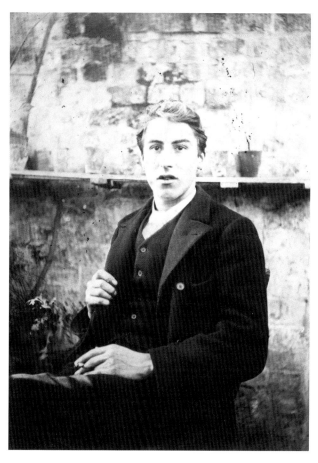

⬆ Portrait of George Edward
Stanhope Molyneux Herbert,
Fifth Earl of Carnarvon, aged 25.

⬀ Photograph of Howard Carter
aged 17.

Carnarvon sought to employ his own archaeologist, and in 1907 the
Director of the Egyptian Antiquities Service recommended to him a certain
Howard Carter.

The youngest of 11 children, Howard Carter spent much of his childhood
in the small Norfolk town of Swaffham. He came to Egyptology through
his skills as an artist and excellent draughtsman. In 1891, at the age of 17,
Carter was engaged by the British Egyptologist Percy Edward Newberry
to ink line drawings of wall reliefs and inscriptions for a publication by the
Egypt Exploration Fund. That same year he travelled to Egypt as Newberry's
assistant to help record the ancient tombs at Beni Hasan, and it was from
there, in January 1892, that Carter joined Flinders Petrie's expedition at
Tell el-Amarna. He was subsequently employed by the Egypt Exploration
Fund as an archaeological draughtsman and by the Egyptian government
as Inspector of Monuments, first at Luxor and later at Saqqara.

Carter accepted Carnarvon's offer of a job in 1907 and so began several
years of productive excavation funded by the earl. The ultimate aim of
the two men, however, was to explore the Valley of the Kings at Thebes
and, when the concession to work there became available in 1914, Lord
Carnarvon seized the opportunity. They were both convinced that there
were yet more tombs to be discovered, including that of Tutankhamun.

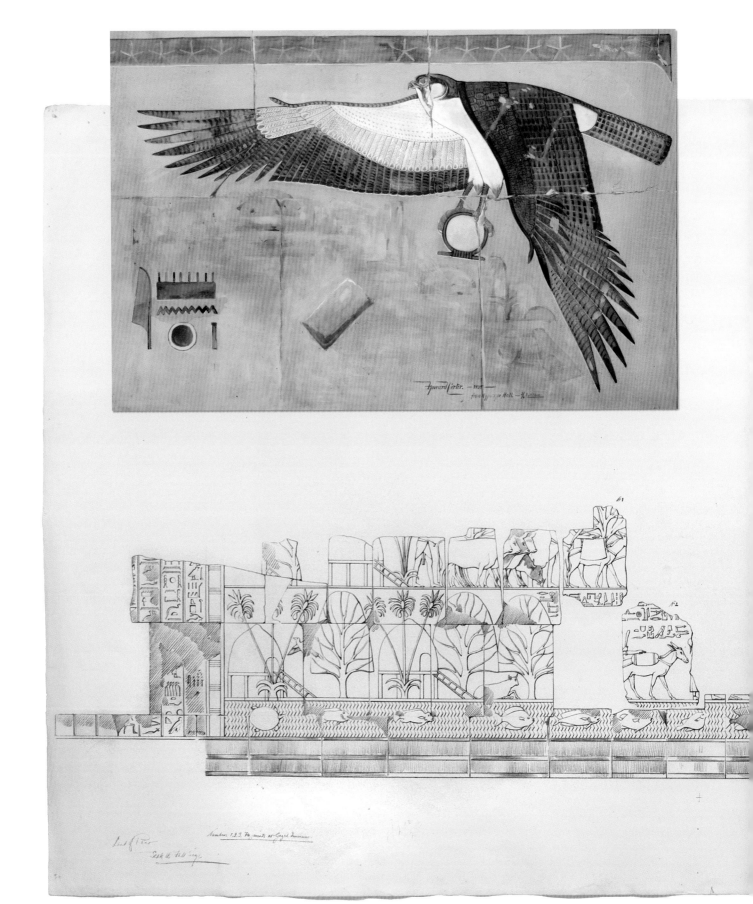

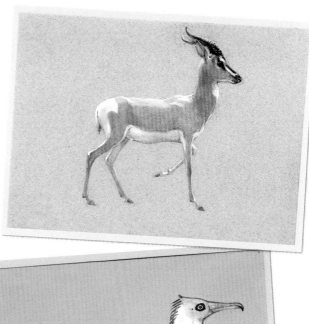

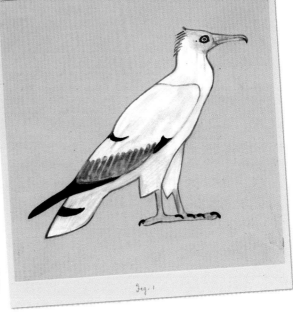

◐ Howard Carter's watercolour copy of a painted scene showing the Horus falcon (left) and his pencil facsimile of the 'Punt relief' from the mortuary temple of Queen Hatshepsut at Deir el-Bahri (centre).

◐ Carter's study of a Dorcas gazelle and a painted hieroglyph of an Egyptian vulture from a tomb.

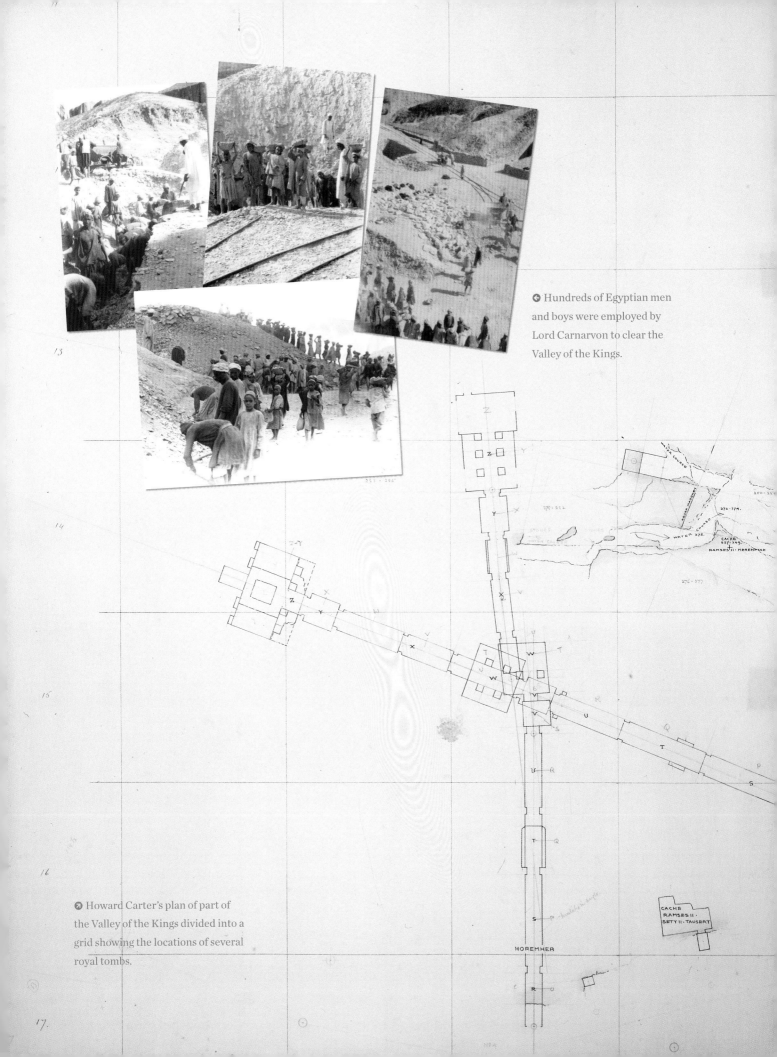

◐ Hundreds of Egyptian men
and boys were employed by
Lord Carnarvon to clear the
Valley of the Kings.

◒ Howard Carter's plan of part of
the Valley of the Kings divided into a
grid showing the locations of several
royal tombs.

The Search for Tutankhamun

Years of excavation and exploration had transformed the Valley into a tourist destination, with open tombs surrounded by thousands of tons of dirt and limestone rubble that had been piled in dumps by earlier archaeologists. These vast spoil heaps covered parts of the Valley that had never been properly examined and, in any search for further tombs, they would have to first be cleared. Before the advent of mechanical diggers, archaeologists were dependent on manual labour for such a task. Hundreds of Egyptian men and boys could be employed relatively inexpensively; once furnished with adzes and baskets, they would move debris to new dumps or into trucks on rails to be carried further away. This was slow, hard, back-breaking work.

In order to excavate the ground in an organised manner, Carter divided the Valley into a grid system and cleared a single square at a time. Progress was interrupted, however, by the outbreak of the First World War, and significant work could only resume in 1917. Three seasons of excavation followed in which as much as 200,000 tons of sand and stones were moved but without finding a single object of significance. By the summer of 1922, with his financial situation becoming increasingly difficult, Lord Carnarvon decided to terminate the work. In June of that year Carnarvon invited Carter to join him for a weekend at his country home, Highclere Castle in Hampshire, where he intended to convey the bad news. Despondently, the two men spent some time studying a plan of the Valley of the Kings, noting in particular a square on the grid that had not been explored in their first season as this would have prevented tourists reaching the open tomb of King Ramesses VI. Carter proposed just one more season to clear the last remaining square. Ever the gambler, Carnarvon agreed.

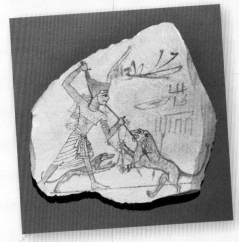

⊕ A limestone ostracon (a piece of stone used for writing or sketches) found by workmen in the search for Tutankhamun's tomb and depicting an unidentified king spearing a lion, about 1186–1070 BC.

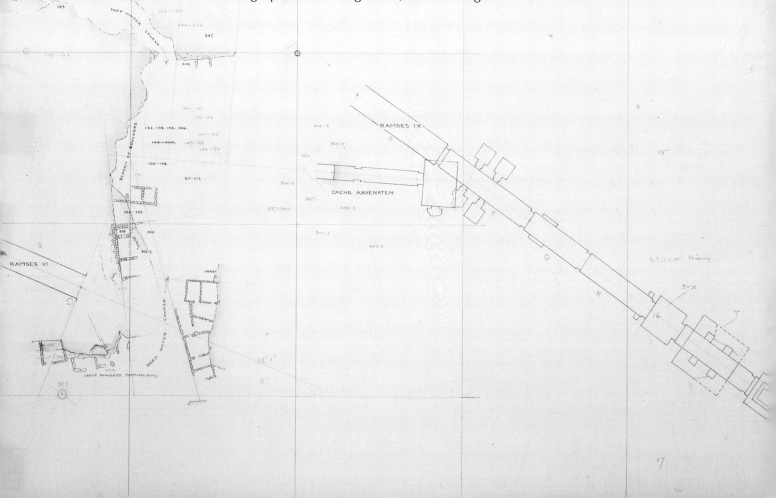

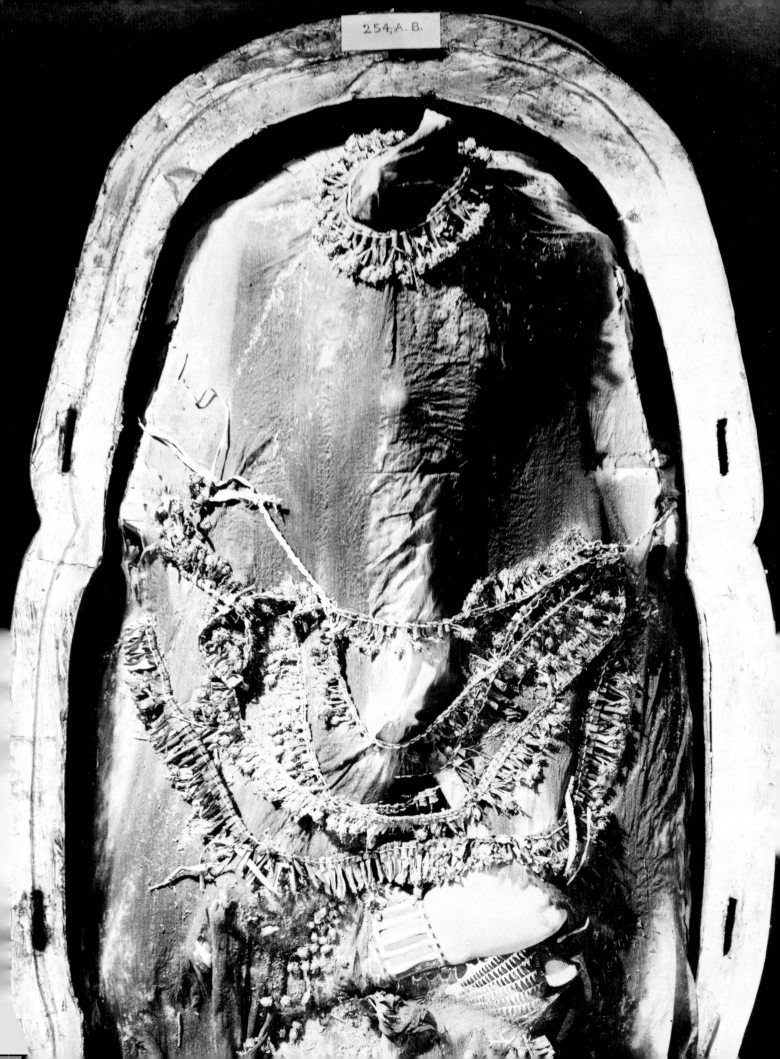

The Discovery of Tutankhamun

*'At last have made wonderful discovery
in Valley; a magnificent tomb with seals
intact; re-covered same for your arrival;
congratulations.'*

E xcavation resumed on 1 November 1922. Three days later the remains of ancient huts used during the construction of the tomb of Ramesses VI were cleared and, as the workmen removed the final stones, they uncovered a step cut into the Valley floor. By 5 November, 12 descending steps had been exposed. Even before the bottom of the stairway had been reached, the upper part of a blocked and plastered doorway was revealed. The plaster was impressed with a range of oval seals, including that of a recumbent jackal over the figures of nine bound foreign captives (the so-called 'necropolis seal', representing the traditional enemies of Egypt), but none on which a name could be read.

On the morning of 6 November, having refilled the staircase with rubble, Carter sent a telegram to Lord Carnarvon who was still in England:

> At last have made wonderful discovery in Valley; a magnificent tomb with seals intact; re-covered same for your arrival; congratulations.

On 24 November Carnarvon, accompanied by his daughter Lady Evelyn Herbert, was present as the staircase was cleared to its full depth of 16 steps. On the lower part of the plastered doorway were seal impressions clearly naming Tutankhamun.

After recording the seal impressions, the blocking of plastered stone was removed, revealing a sloping tunnel completely filled from floor to ceiling with chips of limestone. This debris was cleared and, 9 metres along the tunnel, a second doorway was uncovered, also marked with seals of Tutankhamun. Both outer and inner doorways showed evidence of having been opened and then resealed in antiquity, suggesting that the tomb beyond may have been plundered

◉ Tutankhamun's middle coffin as first revealed, shrouded by linen and covered with garlands of flowers.

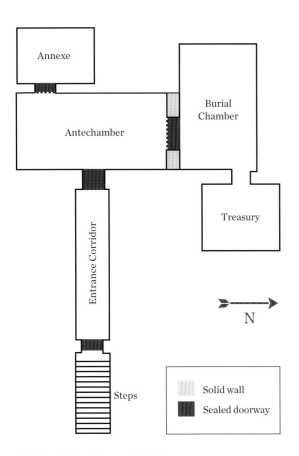

Annexe

Antechamber

Burial Chamber

Treasury

Entrance Corridor

Steps

N

Solid wall

Sealed doorway

⬆ Plan of Tutankhamun's tomb.

⬇ Measured perspective drawing
of Tutankhamun's tomb by
Harold Parkinson (1918–1995).

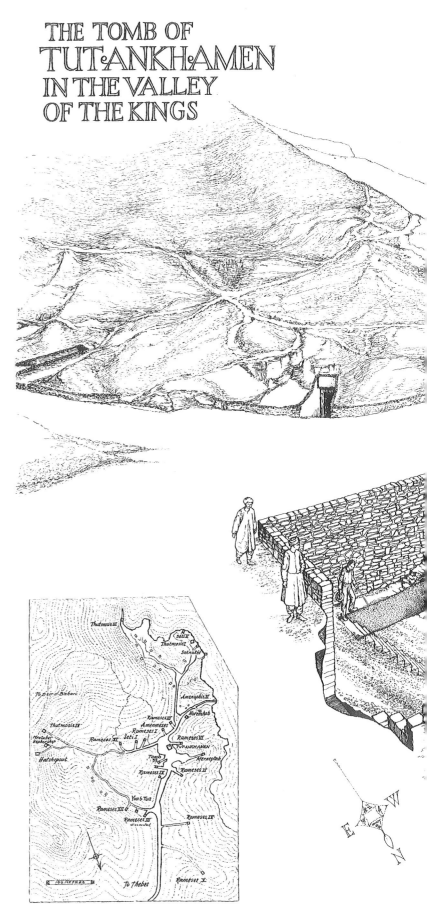

THE TOMB OF
TUT·ANKH·AMEN
IN THE VALLEY
OF THE KINGS

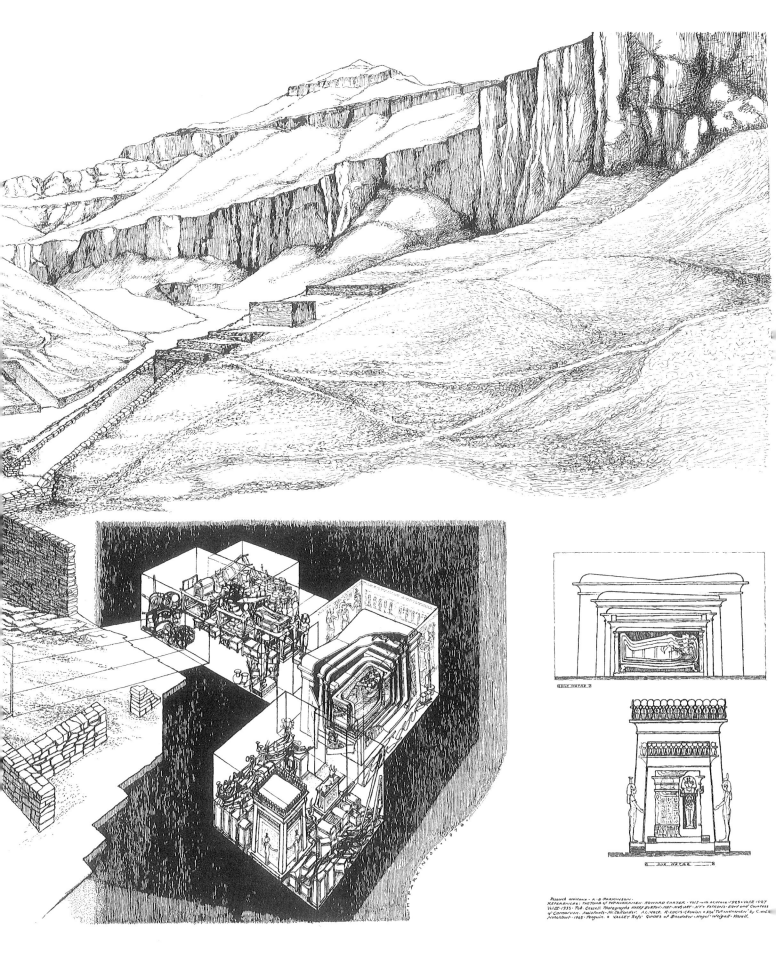

on several occasions; indeed, several objects that had presumably been dropped at the tomb's entrance by robbers were found among the rubble filling the corridor.

On the afternoon of 26 November Carter prepared to open the second doorway. Joined by Lord Carnarvon, Lady Herbert, and his friend Arthur Callender, Carter levered out some of the stones at the top. He captures the excitement of this moment in his notes:

Candles were procured – the all important tell-tale for foul gases when opening an ancient subterranean excavation – I widened the breach and by means of the candle looked in, while Ld. C., Lady E, and Callender with the Reises [Egyptian foremen of the workers] waited in anxious expectation. It was sometime before one could see, the hot air escaping caused the candle to flicker, but as soon as one's eyes became accustomed to the glimmer of light the interior of the chamber gradually loomed before one, with its strange and wonderful medley of extraordinary and beautiful objects heaped upon one another. There was naturally short suspense for those present who could not see, when Lord Carnarvon said to me 'Can you see anything'.

◑ 'Discovered tomb under tomb of Ramses VI Investigated same & found seals intact' Howard Carter's diary entry for 5 November 1922.

◑ Howard Carter's journal entry for 26 November 1922 recording the opening of the door leading to the tomb's Antechamber.

 177 11th Month **NOVEMBER 1922** 30 Days	30 Days **NOVEMBER 1922** 11th Month 178
5 SUNDAY [309—56] 21 after Trinity *Discovered tomb under tomb of Ramses VI. Investigated Same + found Seals intact.*	**7 TUESDAY** [311—54]
6 MONDAY [310—55] 	**8 WEDNESDAY** [312—53]

(Nov. 26 Continued)

It was sometime before one could see, the hot air escaping caused the candle to flicker, but as soon as one's eyes became accustomed to the glimmer of light the interior of the chamber gradually loomed before one, with its strange and wonderful medley of extraordinary and beautiful objects heaped upon one another. There was naturally short suspense for those present who could not see, when Lord Carnarvon said to me "Can you see anything?" I replied to him Yes, it is wonderful. I then with precaution made the hole sufficiently large for both of us to see. With the light of an electric torch as well as an additional candle we looked in. Our sensations and astonishment are difficult to describe as the better light revealed to us the marvellous collection of treasures: two strange ebony-black effigies of a King, gold sandalled, bearing staff and mace, loomed out from the cloak of darkness; gilded couches in strange forms, lion-headed, Hathor-headed, and beast infernal; exquisitely painted, inlaid, and ornamental caskets; flowers; alabaster vases, some beautifully executed of lotus and papyrus twice; strange black shrines with a gilded monster appearing from within; quite ordinary looking white chests; finely carved chairs; a golden inlaid throne; a heap of large curious white oviform boxes; beneath our very eyes, on the threshold, a lovely lotiform wishing-cup in translucent alabaster; stools of all shapes and design, of both common and rare material; and, lastly a confusion of over turned ~~parts~~ chariots glinting with gold, peering from amongst which was a ~~manufacture the furniture~~ (of a vanished civilization) The first ~~was~~ impression of which suggests the property-room of an Opera ~~house~~. Our sensations were bewildering and full of strange emotion. We questioned one another as to the meaning of it all. Was it a tomb or merely a cache? A sealed-doorway between the two sentinel statues proved there was more beyond, and with the numerous cartouches bearing the name of Tut-Ankh-Amen on most of the objects before us, there was little doubt that there behind was the grave of that Pharaoh.

We closed the hole, locked the wooden-grill which has been placed upon the first-doorway, we mounted our donkeys and return home contemplating what we had seen.

Advised the Chief Inspector of the Antiquity Department, who was with us at the commencement of the opening of the first doorway, and asked him to come as soon as possible, preferably the following afternoon to enable us to prepare an electrical installation for careful inspection of this extraordinary and pleasing discovery.

(Snake)

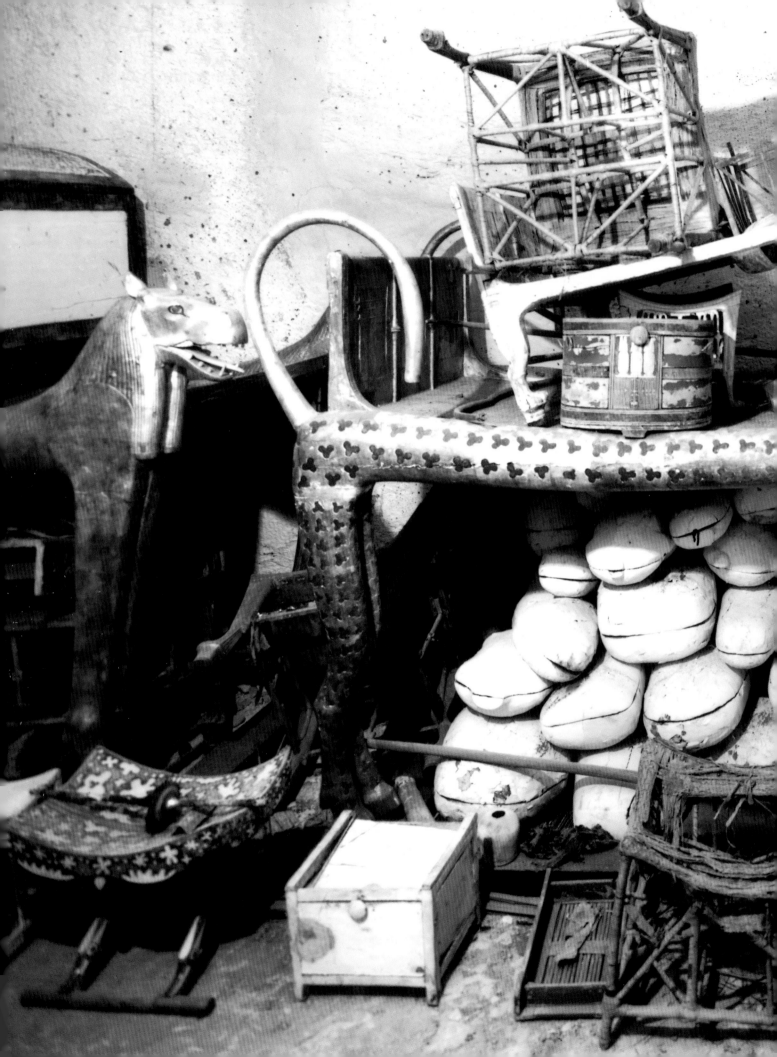

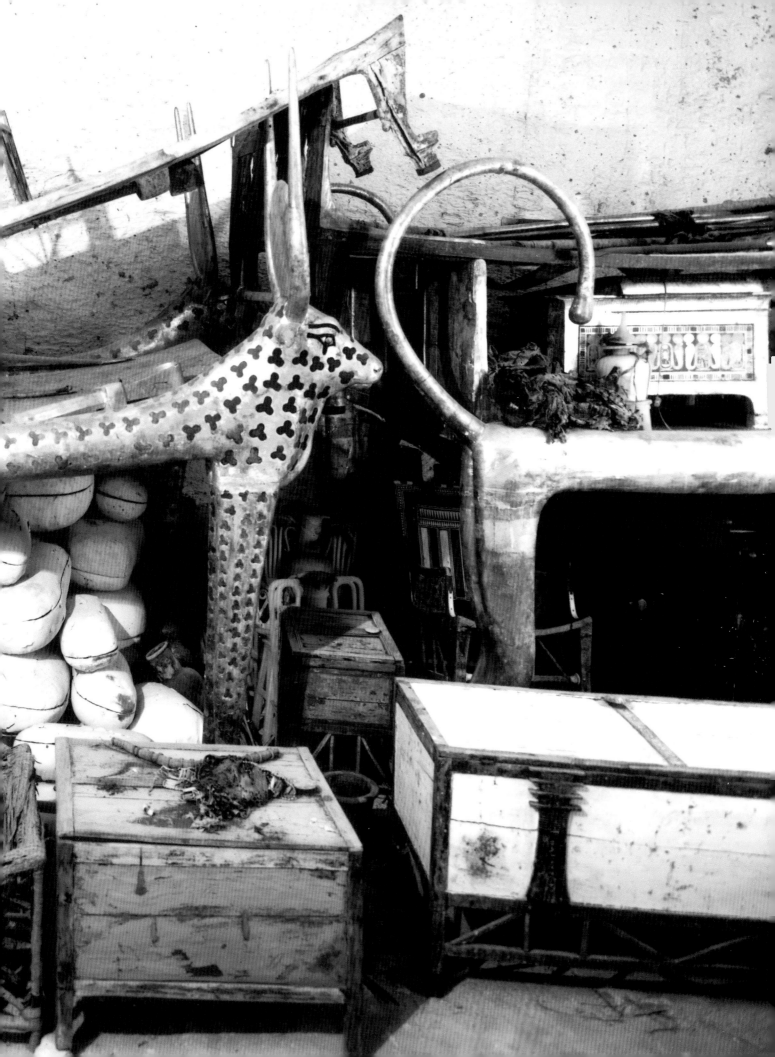

'Can you see anything?'

I replied to him Yes, it is wonderful.

Carter (or possibly his colleague Arthur Mace) developed this description for publication in *The Tomb of Tut.Ankh.Amen*:

Candle tests were applied as a precaution against possible foul gases, and then, widening the hole a little, I inserted the candle and peered in, Lord Carnarvon, Lady Evelyn and Callender standing anxiously beside me to hear the verdict. At first I could see nothing, the hot air escaping from the chamber causing the candle flame to flicker, but presently, as my eyes grew accustomed to the light, details of the room within emerged slowly from the mist, strange animals, statues, and gold – everywhere the glint of gold. For the moment – an eternity it must have seemed to the others standing by – I was struck dumb with amazement, and when Lord Carnarvon, unable to stand the suspense any longer, inquired anxiously, 'Can you see anything?' it was all I could do to get out the words, 'Yes, wonderful things.'

'Yes, wonderful things.'

With the contents of the Antechamber revealed, Lord Carnarvon wrote a letter, postmarked 28 November 1922, to the Egyptologist Alan Gardiner, in which he captures the almost breathless thrill of discovery:

The find is extraordinary it is a cache & has been plundered to a certain extent but even the ancients could not completely destroy it After some slight plundering the inspectors shut it again. So far it is Tutankamon beds boxes & every conceivable thing there is a box with a few papyri in – the throne of the King the most marvellous inlaid chair you ever saw –

2 life size figures of the King bituminised – all sorts of religious signs hardly known up to date The King clothing rotten but gorgeous. Everything is in a very ticklish state owing to constant handlings & openings in ancient times (I reckon on having to spend 2000£ on preserving & packing) The most wonderful ushabti in wood of the King wood portrait head ditto endless staves etc Some with most wonderful work 4 chariots

The most miraculous alabaster vases ever seen

3 colossal beds of honour with extraordinary animals

There is a further room so packed one cannot see really what is there – Some of the boxes are marvellous chairs innumerable a wonderful stool ebony & ivory

Then there is a bricked up room which we have not yet opened Probably containing the mummies I should not be surprised to find therein Tut & his wife & Smenkara & his, but so far its all Tut.

There is enough stuff to fill the whole Egyptian section upstairs of the B.M. [British Museum]

Objects stacked along the west wall of the Antechamber. Modern digital colourisation of Harry Burton's original black and white photograph.

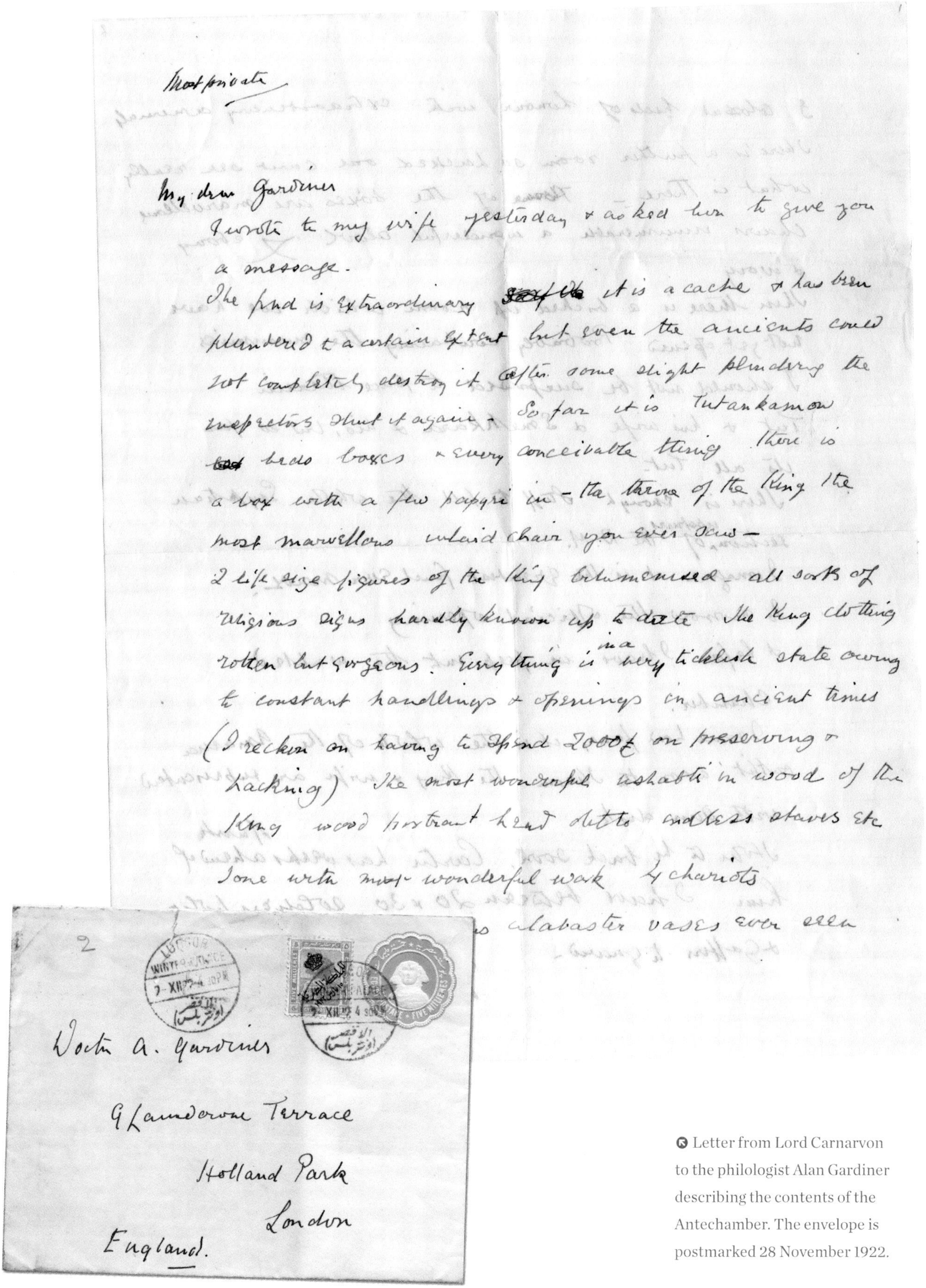

Most private

My dear Gardiner

I wrote to my wife yesterday & asked her to give you a message.

The find is extraordinary ~~itself~~ it is a cache & has been plundered to a certain extent but even the ancients could not completely destroy it after some slight plundering the inspectors shut it again. So far it is Tutankamon ~~and~~ beds boxes & every conceivable thing there is a box with a few papyri in — the throne of the King the most marvellous inlaid chair you ever saw —

2 life size figures of the King bitumenised all sorts of religious signs hardly known up to date the King clothing rotten but gorgeous. Everything is in a very ticklish state owing to constant handlings & openings in ancient times (I reckon on having to spend 2000£ on preserving & packing) The most wonderful ushabti in wood of the King wood portrait head ditto endless staves etc

Some with most wonderful work 4 chariots ..... alabaster vases ever seen

Docter A. Gardiner

9 Lansdowne Terrace

Holland Park

London

England.

Letter from Lord Carnarvon to the philologist Alan Gardiner describing the contents of the Antechamber. The envelope is postmarked 28 November 1922.

I imagine it is the greatest find ever made.

Tomorrow the official opening & before I leave we peep into the walled Chamber.

I somehow fancy it is the whole of the Amarna outfit as on the throne the King & wife are represented with sun disk

I hope to be back soon. Carter has weeks of work ahead of him I have between 20 & 30 soldiers police & gaffirs to guard.

Yours C.

Unpacking and Recording the Tomb

The task that now confronted Carter was daunting. He was by nature and training an extremely meticulous archaeologist, and he knew that every object had to be accurately recorded before it could be moved from the tomb. In addition, it was clear that much conservation work was also necessary. Carter turned for help to his colleagues in the Egyptian Expedition of the Metropolitan Museum of Art, New York, sending early in December 1922 the following request to the Curator, Albert Lythgoe:

'Discovery colossal and need every assistance. Could you consider loan of Burton in recording in time being? Costs to us. Immediate reply would oblige. Every regards, Carter.'

From 1906 the Expedition had been conducting excavations at several sites, including western Thebes, and a section had been created to record the discoveries in facsimile paintings and photographs. In this close-knit international community of Egyptologists, the Metropolitan Museum was all too willing to help:

'Only too delighted to assist in every possible way. Please call upon Burton and any other members of our staff. Am cabling Burton to that effect. Lythgoe.'

The Excavation Team

Henry ('Harry') Burton (1879–1940) was born in Stamford, Lincolnshire, and received his education through Robert Cust, a scholar of the Italian Renaissance. Burton developed his skill as a photographer while working as Cust's secretary in Florence, and it was there that he met Theodore Davis. Eventually Davis hired Burton, first as his photographer and later as the director of his excavations. When Davis gave up his concession to excavate in the Valley of the Kings in 1914, Burton was hired as photographer for the Metropolitan Museum's Egyptian Expedition.

Harry Burton's glass negatives are among the greatest treasures now housed in the Griffith Institute at Oxford (a second set is held by the Metropolitan Museum of Art, New York). An invaluable record of the excavation, Burton documented the stage-by-stage process in such a way that today the context of every object can be reconstructed in considerable detail. He was a superb photographer able to produce extraordinarily clear and informative photographs, often under very difficult circumstances. Indeed, many of his pictures from the tomb of Tutankhamun are among the finest archaeological photographs ever produced. Burton's attention to lighting and composition reflect his training in fine art photography, and make the images works of art in their own right.

◔ The excavation team (from left to right): Arthur Callender, Arthur Mace, Harry Burton, Howard Carter, Alan Gardiner and Alfred Lucas. The photograph may have been taken by Lord Carnarvon.

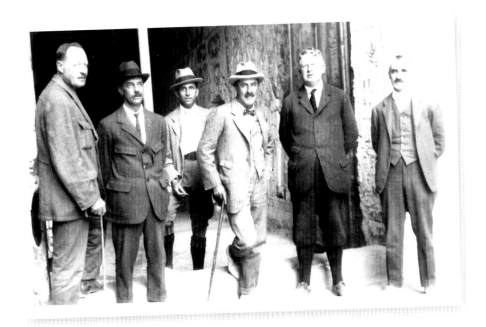

Arthur Cruttenden Mace (1874–1928), the Metropolitan Museum's Associate Curator of Egyptian Art, also an Englishman, was an experienced Egyptologist who helped with conservation and co-authored the official account of the discovery. He left the excavation and Egypt in 1924 as his health deteriorated.

Arthur Robert ('Pecky') Callender (1875–1936) was a retired architect and engineer and a good friend of Carter. He was invited to join the excavation at the beginning of November 1922. Callender's skills would prove invaluable especially during the dismantling and removal of the large gilded shrines from Tutankhamun's burial chamber.

Alfred Lucas (1867–1945) was at the time of the discovery Director of the Chemical Department of the Egyptian Government, and subsequently, from 1923–1932, worked as a consultant Chemist to the Egyptian

Antiquities Service. He was responsible for giving scientific advice and for object conservation and restoration, establishing a field laboratory in the neighbouring tomb of Seti II. Lucas's experience in conserving the objects from Tutankhamun's tomb contributed much to his ground-breaking publication *Ancient Egyptian Materials and Industries*, first published in 1926.

Walter Hauser (1893–1959) and **Lindsley Foote Hall** (1883–1969) helped produce plans and scale drawings of the tomb. Both men found Carter a difficult man to work for and ended their association with the excavation after making a plan showing the arrangement of objects in the Antechamber.

Percy Edward Newberry (1868–1949), Honorary Reader in Egyptian Art at Liverpool University, was especially interested in the botanical remains recovered from the tomb.

Alan Henderson Gardiner (1879–1963), the leading philologist of his generation, recorded all the ancient texts found in the tomb.

James Henry Breasted (1865–1935) was director of the Oriental Institute of the University of Chicago and a renowned historian. His work on the tomb focused largely on the doorway seal impressions.

Timeline of the Excavation

A lesser archaeologist would have rapidly cleared the tomb, but Carter took this responsibility extremely seriously. As a result, the process of recording, removal and conservation of the contents took a decade to complete.

1922	**4 November:** first step leading to the tomb discovered **5 November:** outer doorway revealed **26 November:** access hole made in inner doorway leading to Antechamber **29 November:** official opening of Antechamber and Annexe **27 December:** first object, Painted Box no.21, removed from Antechamber	1925	**29 January:** work resumes **13 October:** cover of the first coffin removed **23 October:** cover of the second coffin removed **28 October:** cover of the final coffin removed and the mummy is exposed **11 November:** start of unwrapping Tutankhamun's mummy
1923	**9 January:** Contract signed with *The Times* **16 February:** the Burial Chamber is officially opened **5 April:** Lord Carnarvon dies	1926	**24 October:** work starts in the Treasury
		1927	**30 October:** work starts in the Annexe
		1930	**10 November:** final objects removed from the tomb
1924	**12 February:** sarcophagus lid lifted **13 February:** political problems halt work	1932	**Spring:** conservation work completed and final objects sent to Cairo

The Process of Recovery

Carter developed a methodical procedure for recording and removing all 5,398 artefacts found in the tomb. Each object, or group of objects, was given a reference number from 1 to 620; objects within a numbered group were subdivided using single or multiple letters, with bracketed Arabic numerals allowing for further subdivision. Unusually, the final group of objects from the Annexe, numbered as 620, was divided not by letters but by numbers, from 1 to 123.

Key to the recording process was photography. Harry Burton took photographs of objects exactly where they were found, both with and without reference number cards. For group shots, several photographs were taken from different angles in order to record every object at least once. Given the size of the tomb and the density of the material with which it was filled, setting up the cumbersome camera equipment was often a difficult operation. The oppressive heat and lack of light in the tomb also created significant problems; the latter was helped by the use of two movable electric arc lamps, which allowed greater control than a flash, and occasionally mirrors were employed to create special lighting effects.

⊙ A jumble of objects in the Annexe numbered for recording.

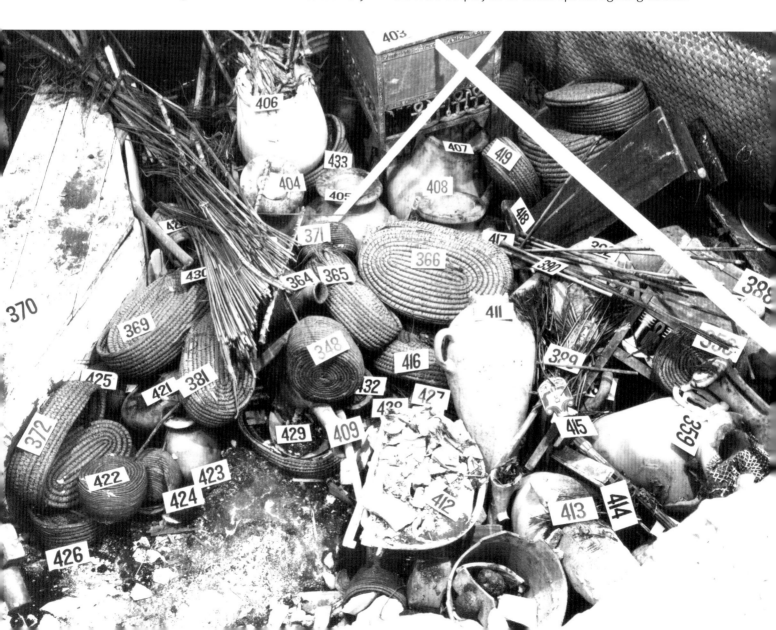

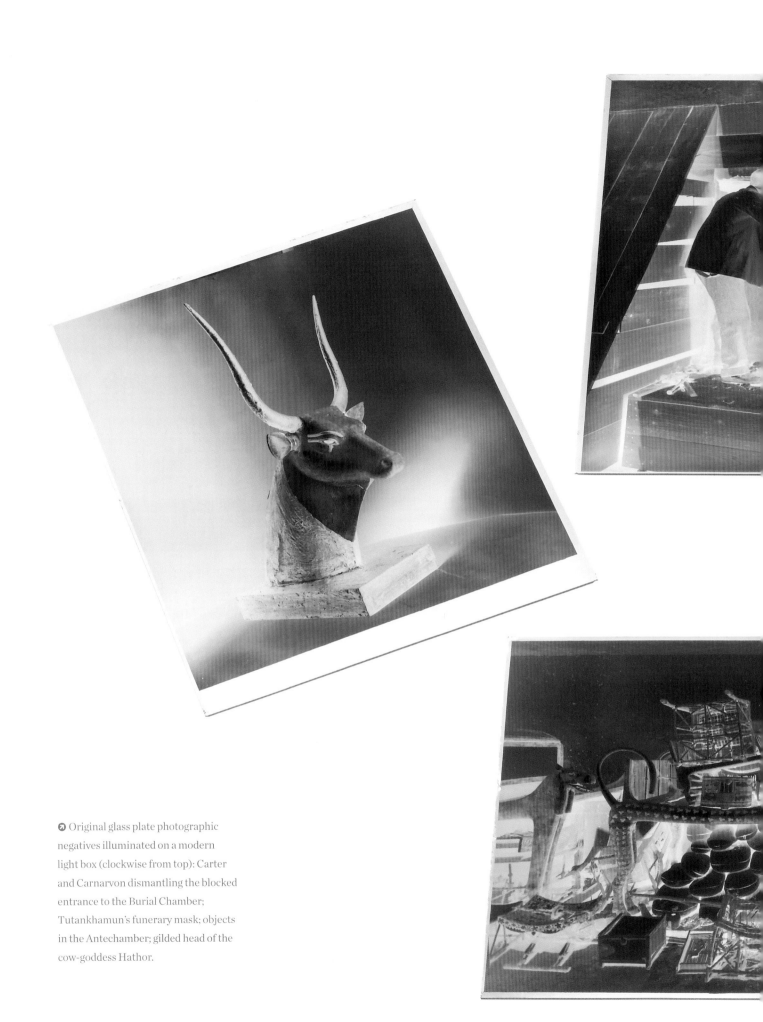

⦿ Original glass plate photographic negatives illuminated on a modern light box (clockwise from top): Carter and Carnarvon dismantling the blocked entrance to the Burial Chamber; Tutankhamun's funerary mask; objects in the Antechamber; gilded head of the cow-goddess Hathor.

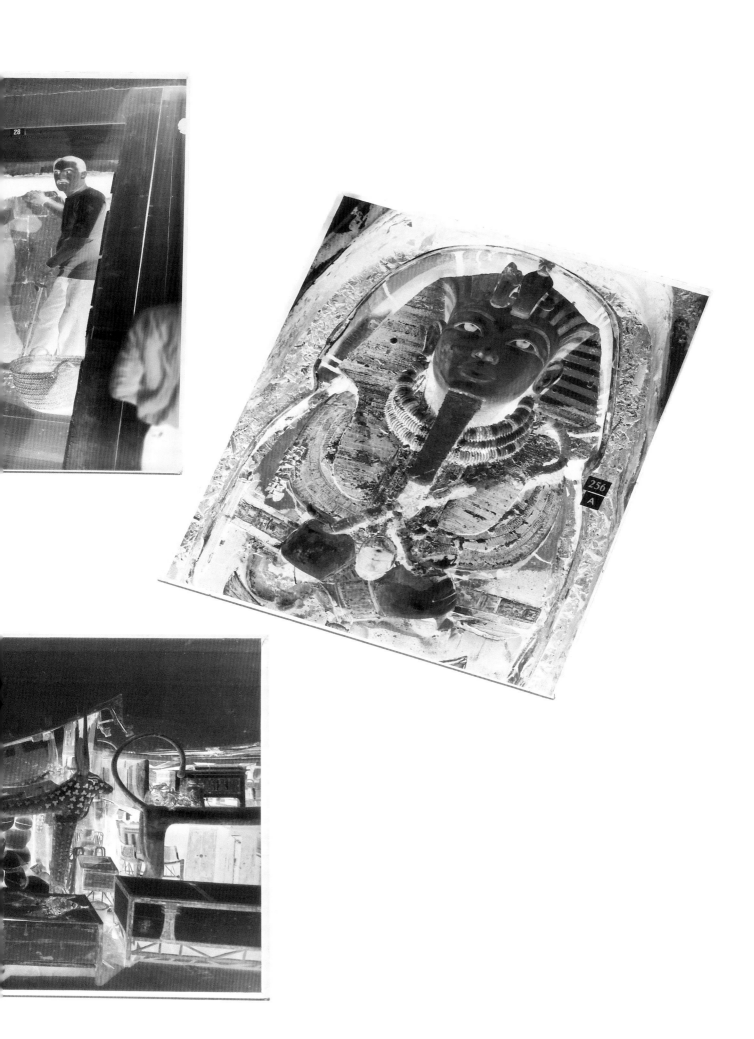

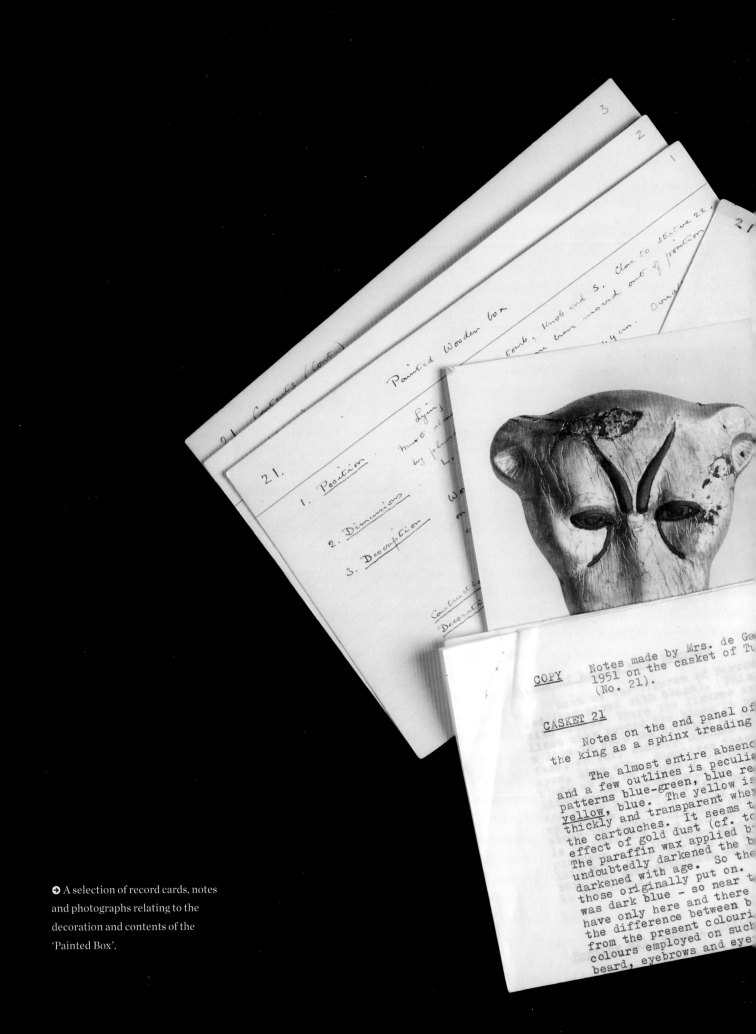

The following text is partially visible on the record cards and notes:

3

2

1

21

21 Contents (contd.)

Painted Wooden Box

tomb. Knob end S. Close to statue 22.

......been moved out of position......

......4 cm.   Overall......

21.   Lying......

1. Position   two alon......
                         by plac......
                         L. ......

2. Dimensions   Woo......
                        on......
3. Description

Construction 21......
Decoration......

COPY   Notes made by Mrs. de Ga......
        1951 on the casket of Tu......
        (No. 21).

CASKET 21

Notes on the end panel of......
the king as a sphinx treading......

The almost entire absenc......
and a few outlines is peculia......
patterns blue-green, blue re......
yellow, blue.   The yellow is......
thickly and transparent wher......
the cartouches.   It seems t......
effect of gold dust (cf. to......
The paraffin wax applied b......
undoubtedly darkened the b......
darkened with age.   So the......
those originally put on.......
was dark blue – so near t......
have only here and there ......
the difference between b......
from the present colouri......
colours employed on such......
beard, eyebrows and eye......

A selection of record cards, notes and photographs relating to the decoration and contents of the 'Painted Box'.

21.

Lid, central line.

Knob end: in midst of winged disk.

Other end: in midst of winged disk.

Band C

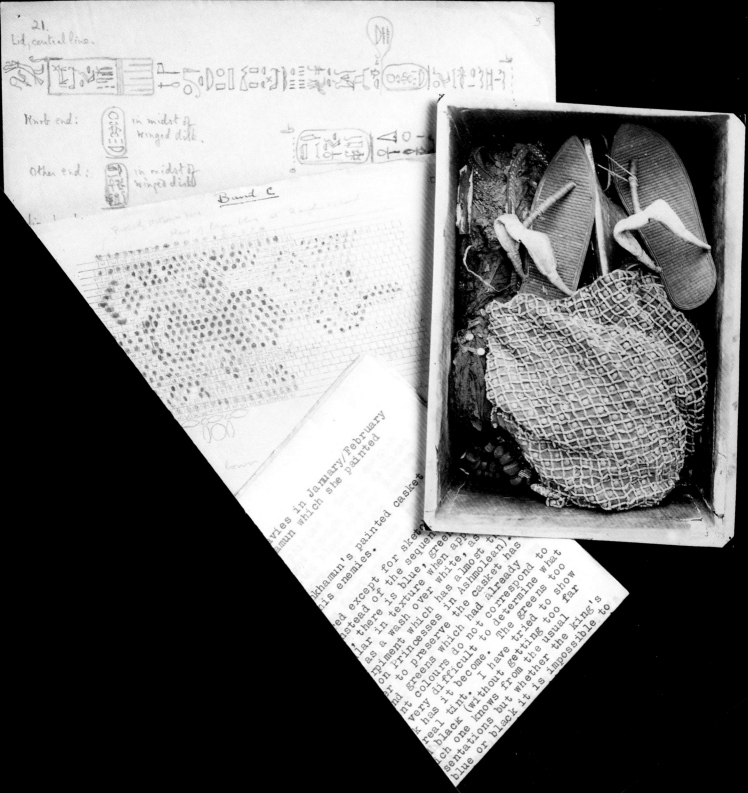

...vies in January/February
...mun which she painted

...khamūn's painted casket
...his enemies.

...ed except for sketch
...stead of the sequen...
...there is blue, green...
...iar in texture when app...
...as a wash over white, as...
...rpiment which has almost t...
...on Princesses in Ashmolean),
...r to preserve the casket has...
...nt colours do not correspond to
...nd greens which had already
...k has it become. The greens show
...very difficult to determine what
...real tint. I have tried too far
...black (without getting too far
...ich one knows from the usual king's
...sentations but whether the king's
...blue or black it is impossible to

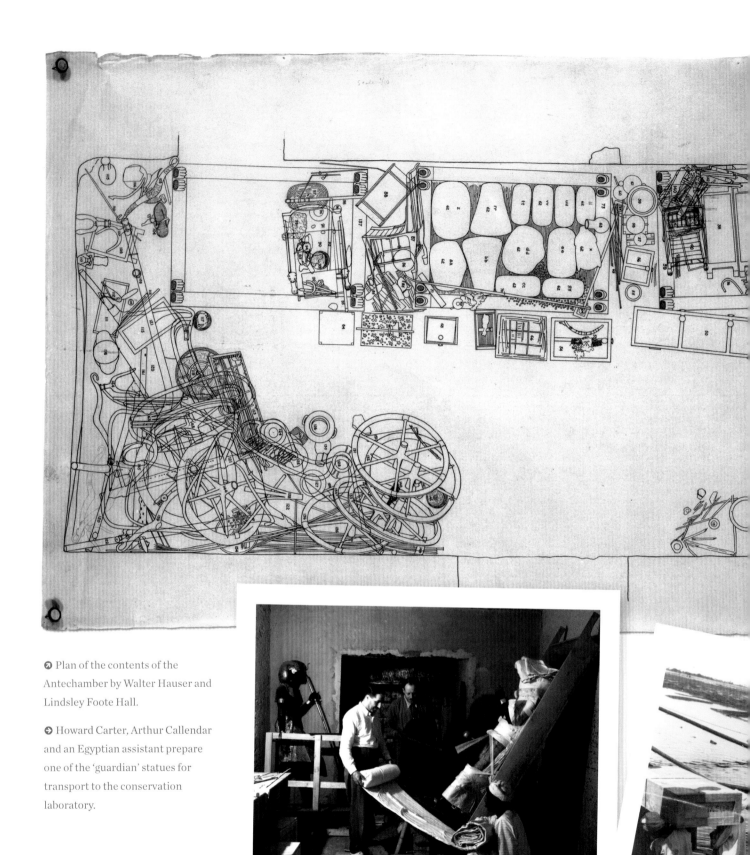

⊙ Plan of the contents of the
Antechamber by Walter Hauser and
Lindsley Foote Hall.

⊙ Howard Carter, Arthur Callendar
and an Egyptian assistant prepare
one of the 'guardian' statues for
transport to the conservation
laboratory.

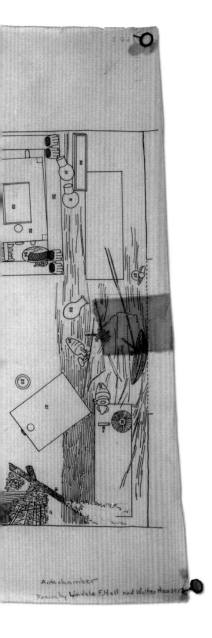

Antechamber
Drawn by Lindsle F. Hall and Walter Hauser

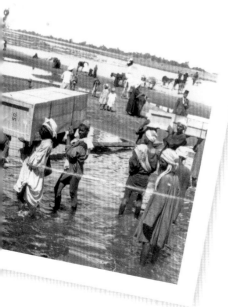

Burton used a large format 'view camera' – a wooden box with a lens, placed on an adjustable tripod. Looking into the camera, the image would have appeared reversed and upside down. The camera lens could be moved backward and forward to focus the image on to a glass plate inside the box. These heavy and fragile glass plates were coated with a light-sensitive mixture of gelatin and silver. A black card, placed between the plate and the lens, was removed to let in the light to expose the image. At this point the timing of the exposure was crucial, all dependant on the skill and judgement of the photographer: too fast and the image would appear light, or under-exposed; too long and the image would be over-exposed. The glass plate was then 'fixed' in a chemical solution, to preserve the negative. Finally a negative could be printed by placing it on to photo-sensitive paper and exposing it to strong light. This was slow and painstaking work requiring a darkroom, for which Burton used a small empty tomb opposite to that of Tutankhamun.

A written description of each object was made by Mace or Carter, sometimes accompanied with an illustration, on a numbered record card. Its location was also marked on a plan of the tomb. Objects were then removed to the conservation laboratory in the tomb of Seti II for treatment by Lucas and Mace, who made further notes on the condition, material and methods of manufacture of many items. After the conservation work was completed, a further photograph was taken. Finally the pieces were wrapped in cotton wadding and strips of calico (cotton cloth) to make them secure for transport in wooden crates, prepared in a carpenter's workshop set up in another adjacent tomb.

As with the search for Tutankhamun, the clearing of his tomb and the transport of objects towards their final home in the Egyptian Museum, Cairo would have been impossible without a vast workforce of Egyptian men and boys. A small Decauville (narrow-gauge) railway was constructed to transport the finds in wheeled trucks, pushed by hand from the tomb entrance towards boats docked on the Nile some 9 kilometres away. However, only a few lengths of railway line were available, so these had to be lifted and re-laid further ahead for each move. With a gang of 50 men it was possible to cover more than half a kilometre an hour, so that each journey from the tomb to the river bank took around 15 hours. This work was carried out in the heat of summer with iron rails that were almost too hot to touch.

Wooden creates containing objects from the tomb are loaded onto a boat for transport along the River Nile to Cairo.

'Wonderful Things'

The contents of the tomb were recorded in an exemplary fashion for the time. The following objects have been selected to highlight something of the variety of finds, as well as the challenges faced by the excavators in documentation, conservation, and interpretation.

The 'Painted Box'

The so-called 'Painted Box' – excavation number 21 – was found in the Antechamber and would be the first object to be removed from the tomb (on 27 December 1922). For Carter this was 'one of the greatest artistic treasures', and it continues to be recognised as one of the finest examples of miniature painting from ancient Egypt. The painted scenes, on all four sides of the wooden box as well as the lid, depict Tutankhamun, identified by his name and titles in hieroglyphs, as a warrior and hunter. These are standard images of ancient Egyptian kingship which portrayed the ruler as a strong and triumphant leader, responsible for maintaining the proper order of the cosmos.

On one long side Tutankhamun in his chariot tramples Syrian soldiers and their horses into an entangled heap on the right side of the panel, while on the opposite side of the box Nubians are driven to the left. The king thus defeats the traditional northern and southern enemies of Egypt. On both short sides of the box Tutankhamun is depicted as a pair of sphinxes that crush foreigners underfoot, flanked by oval cartouches containing his names. On the lid the king is twice represented driving a chariot, but here he shoots arrows at desert game moving to the right and lions that flee to the left. The lid would originally have been attached to the box by a cord, the two ends of which would have been wound around one knob on the lid and another on the end of the box, to which a mud seal was then attached.

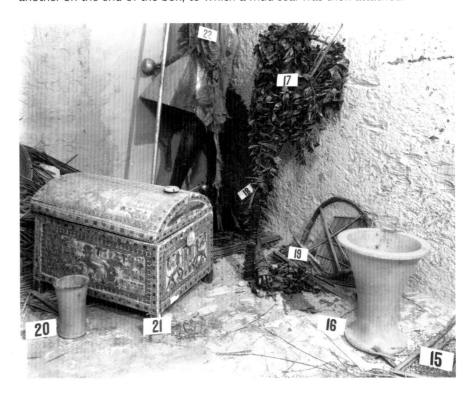

◗ The 'Painted Box', object number 21, soon after its discovery in the Antechamber.

An accurate copy of all four painted sides of the box, as well as the lid, was later made by the artist Nina de Garis Davies (1881–1965). Trained at the Slade School of Fine Art and the Royal College of Art in London, Anna ('Nina') Davies was married to the Egyptologist Norman de Garis Davies, with whom she began a career copying Egyptian tomb paintings, particularly in the region of Thebes. By using egg tempera instead of the usual watercolour paint employed by other copyists, she achieved an effect that faithfully echoes the colouring and texture of the original paintings, as well as reproducing areas of damage.

The box contained a range of the king's clothing, including sandals made of rush and papyrus and others of leather and beadwork. There were robes decorated with gold and faience sequins, a fine linen glove, and a leopard-skin cloak. A beautiful beaded robe lying at the top of the pile sadly crumbled as it was removed. In the absence of colour photography, the bright colours of other beaded garments were recorded on record cards. It took Mace and Lucas three weeks to empty the box of its contents – a test of their skill that proved invaluable for subsequent work on the objects from the tomb.

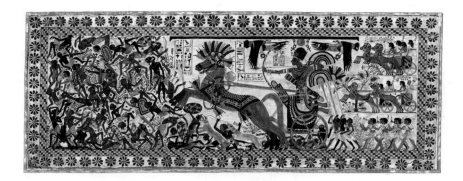

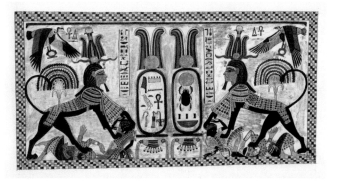

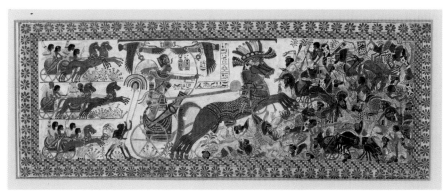

❷ Watercolour facsimiles by Nina de Garis Davies of side panels of the 'Painted Box'.

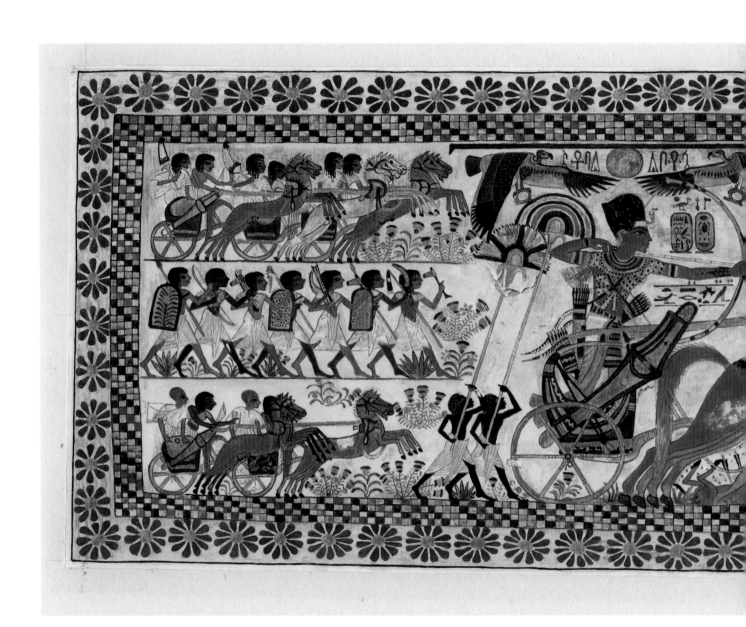

⬆ Watercolour facsimile by Nina de Garis Davies of a panel on the lid of the 'Painted Box'.

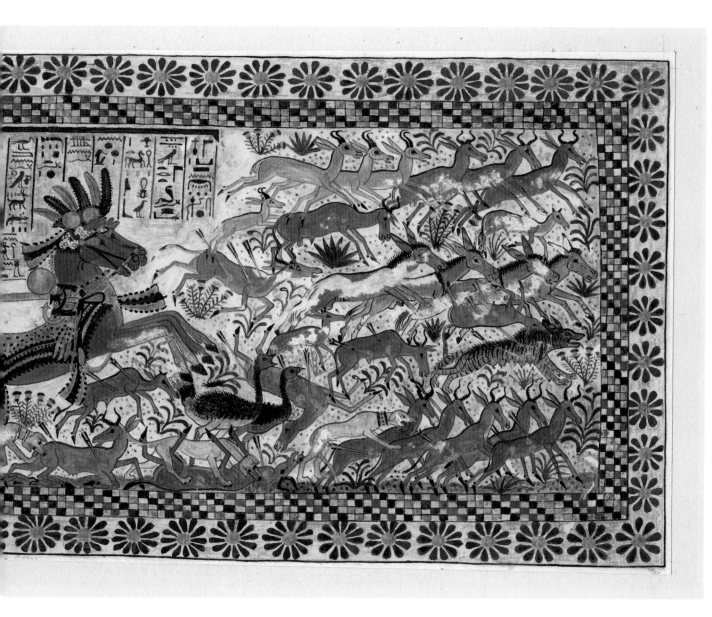

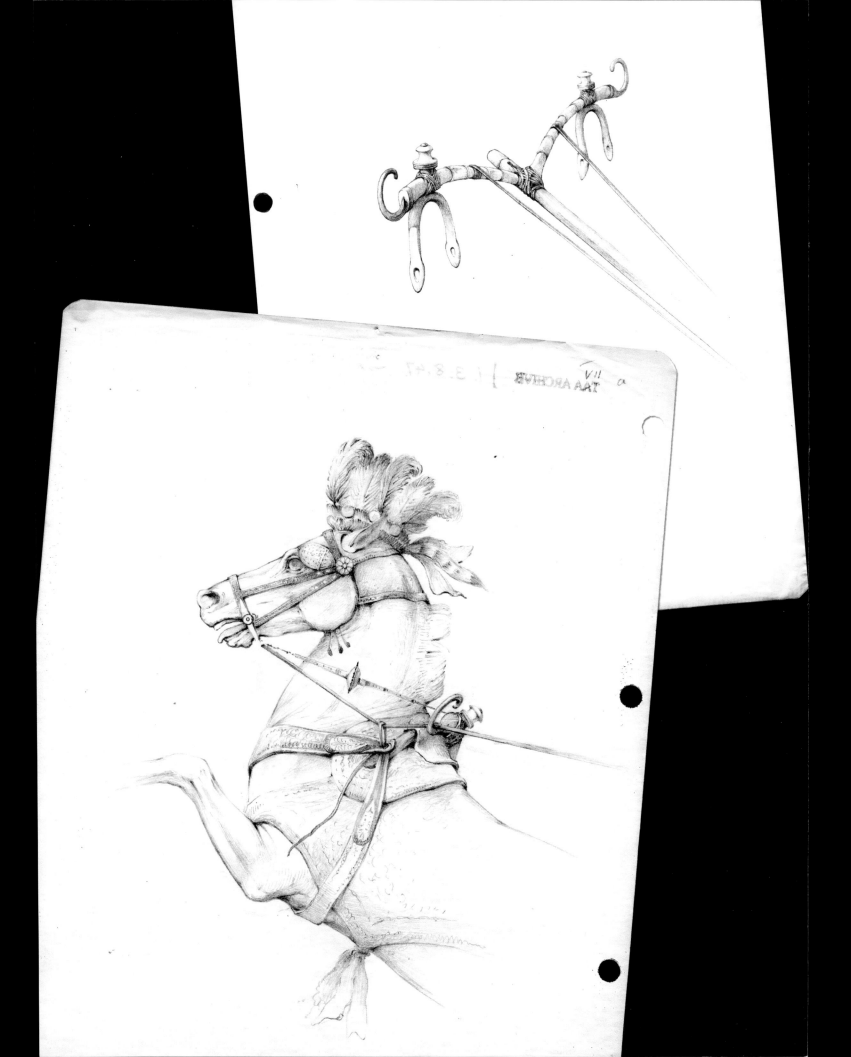

TAA ARCHIVE | 13.8.47 | VII a

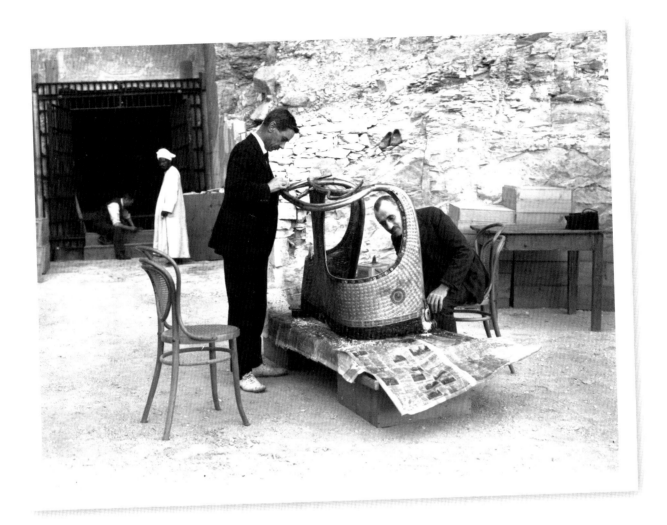

🔄 Drawing by Howard Carter of a
chariot yoke and his reconstruction
of the harness of a chariot horse.

⬆ Arthur Mace (left) and Alfred
Lucas (right) treating the body of
a chariot.

Chariots and Horse Trappings

The dynamic imagery on the Painted Box reflects the importance of chariots as symbols of Egyptian kingship by the time of Tutankhamun's reign, the horse and chariot having been introduced to Egypt around 1600 BC. Tutankhamun's tomb contained six chariots – four were found at the southeast end of the Antechamber and another two along the north wall of the Treasury. The chariots posed significant challenges for recording and conservation as they had been dismantled in order to fit into the tomb, and the various pieces were stacked in disordered heaps. The two finest vehicles, which Carter identified as the king's 'state chariots', were built from a wooden body, covered with gesso (a type of plaster) overlaid with gold, and highlighted with coloured inlays of glass and stone. Two of the chariots appear to be lighter vehicles, perhaps designed for hunting. Carter was clearly fascinated by the construction of not only the chariots, but also the yokes and harnesses used to attach the elaborately bedecked stallions, and he employed his considerable skills as an artist to reconstruct their original appearance and function.

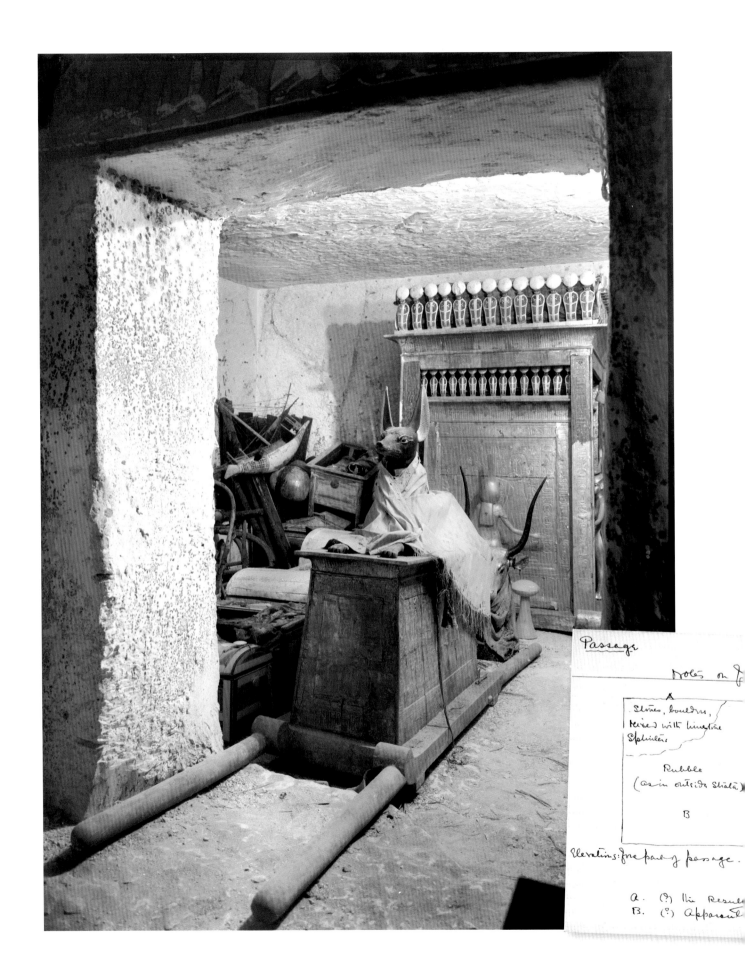

The King's Jewellery

Some 200 items of jewellery were found in the tomb, with the greatest concentration in the Treasury within a portable wooden shrine surmounted by a majestic figure of the jackal-god Anubis, as well as two further caskets. The jewellery ranged from simple necklaces and bracelets to elaborate collars and pectorals. It was fashioned from gold, electrum, silver, bronze, and iron, with the finest examples inlaid with colourful stones and artificial materials such as 'Egyptian blue' and glass. Some pieces were probably prepared specifically for the tomb while others had been worn in life, several by Tutankhamun's predecessors whose names are represented in hieroglyphs among the designs of the jewellery.

The artist Winifred Brunton (1880–1959) was the wife of British Egyptologist Guy Brunton, who was appointed as Assistant Keeper of the Cairo Museum in 1931. Mrs Brunton may have seen the jewellery from Tutankhamun's tomb at first hand and she copied certain pieces in gouache paint on ivory, capturing the luminosity of their original vibrant colours. She is best known for her two-volume book of imaginative portrait paintings *Kings and Queens of Ancient Egypt* (1926) and *Great Ones of Ancient Egypt* (1929), which also included depictions of Tutankhamun and his wife Ankhesenamun, as well as King Akhenaten and Queen Nefertiti.

The jewellery from box number 267 was especially magnificent. This box was one of more than 50 found in the tomb, many of which had been ransacked by thieves. It was evident from the way in which the blockings to the tomb entrance and the inner chambers had been re-sealed that in the years following the burial there had been two break-ins. Following the first robbery, the tomb was closed by filling the entrance corridor with stone rubble. In a second break-in thieves had tunnelled through the

◐ Entrance to the Treasury, guarded by a portable shrine surmounted by the jackal god Anubis.

◑ Record card with a diagram of the filling of the entrance corridor documenting evidence for robbers (left) and another with a drawing of a pendant recovered from the tomb (right).

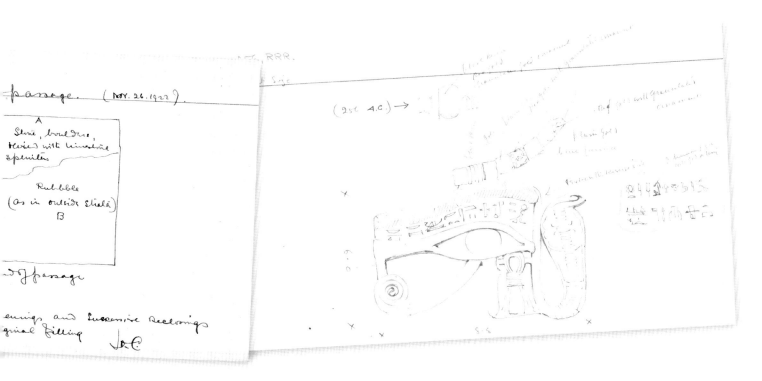

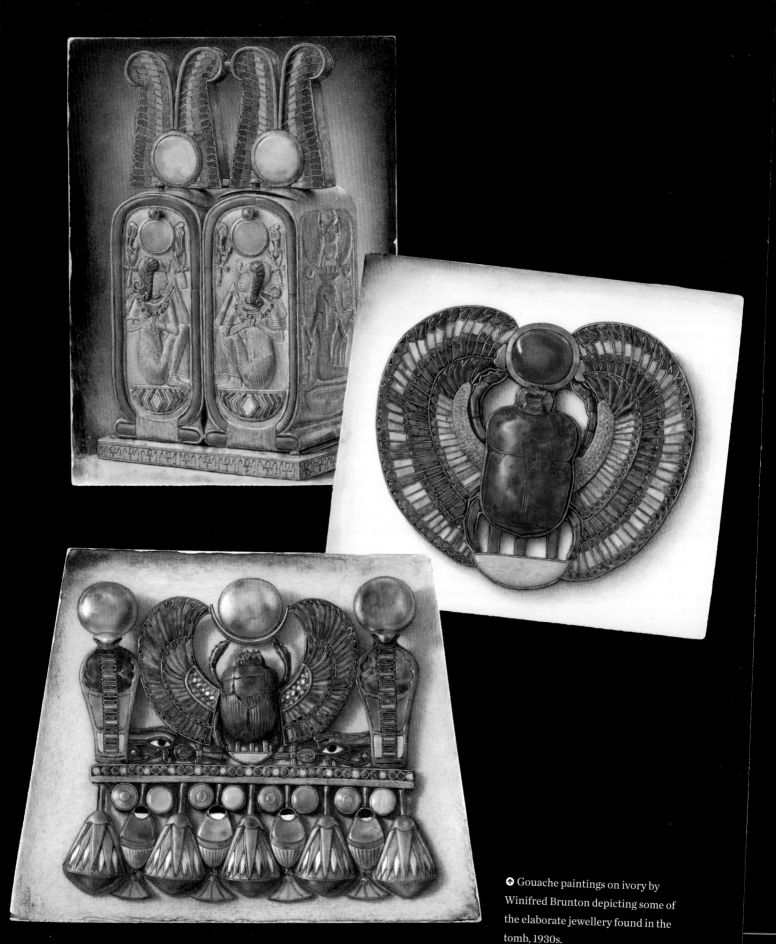

⊙ Gouache paintings on ivory by
Winifred Brunton depicting some of
the elaborate jewellery found in the
tomb, 1930s.

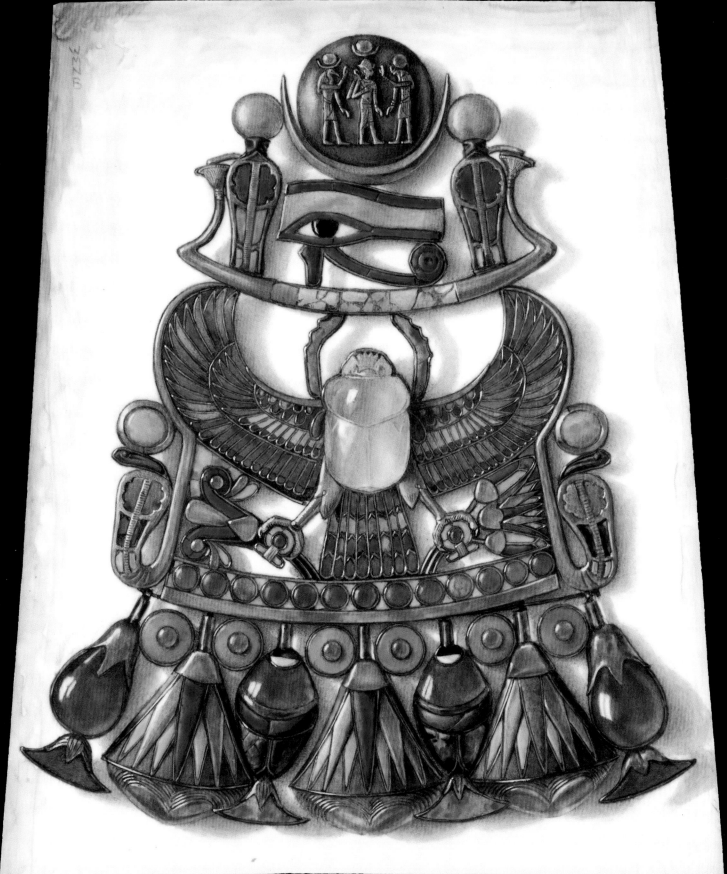

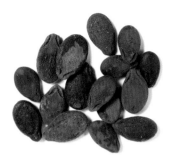

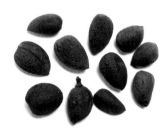

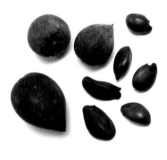

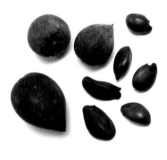

↑ Botanical samples sent for analysis to the Royal Botanic Gardens, Kew (from top to bottom): watermelon, almonds and persea.

corridor fill to gain entry, and they had opened and plundered the boxes in every chamber. Much of the king's jewellery had been stolen during the second robbery – perhaps as much as 60 per cent of that contained in the Treasury caskets if dockets associated with the boxes listing their original contents are accurate. Having discovered the robbery, officials restored some order to the contents of the tomb, partly repacking the boxes. The robber holes were again repaired and the doorway blockings made good.

Botanical Remains
Mostly containing seeds and food, 116 baskets were left in the tomb for use by the king's spirit in the afterlife. These had been stored originally in the Annexe, but the contents had become scattered throughout the chambers during the robberies described above. Plant remains included emmer wheat, fenugreek, chickpeas, lentils, and types of reed and grass. Among various flavourings and spices were juniper berries, coriander, sesame, and black cumin, while fruits were represented by stoned dates, dom-palm fruit, dried grapes, sycamore figs, almonds, and watermelon seeds. There were even garlands of flowers. One placed around the neck of Tutankhamun's mummy included cornflowers and mayweed that flower in March and April, revealing the likely time of year in which the king was buried.

Percy Newberry was interested especially in such plant material, and he published an account of the finds. Samples were also sent to Leonard Boodle, Assistant Keeper of the Jodrell Laboratory at the Royal Botanic Gardens, Kew in southwest London. Many of Boodle's early identifications were published by Lucas in 1926. After his retirement in 1930, Boodle continued to study the plant material from the tomb and sent the results to Carter. Following Carter's death, the findings were never published: only in the 1990s, after the work by Dr F Nigel Hepper of the Botanic Gardens, where these and new findings made public.

The King's Mummy
Tutankhamun's body was enclosed in a nest of three anthropoid (human-shaped) coffins within a rectangular stone sarcophagus. Although the sarcophagus lid was lifted in February 1924, 18 months would pass before the inner coffins were opened. On 28 October 1925 the solid gold cover of the third coffin was removed and the king's mummy was finally revealed.

The outer ornamentation of the mummy included not only the magnificent golden funerary mask. A black resin scarab was suspended from the neck, and modelled hands made of burnished gold clasping the royal symbols of a crook and flail were attached to the mummy at chest level. Further down the body was a large gold *ba*-bird (representing a manifestation of the deceased king's personality) at the top of a gold band running the length of the body, from which extended four horizontal bands. With the exception of the feet and the front of the mask, the entire mummy had been covered by vast quantities of liquid resins. These had consolidated and blackened with age, effectively gluing together the two inner coffins and the body, making it impossible to separate them. A conventional autopsy of the king's mummy was therefore out of the question. Adding to the problems, the

⊙ Baskets of fruit and seeds found scattered in the Annexe.

⊙ Alfred Lucas's register book in which he recorded samples taken for chemical analysis.

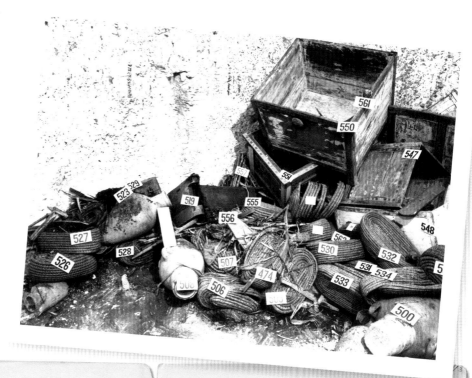

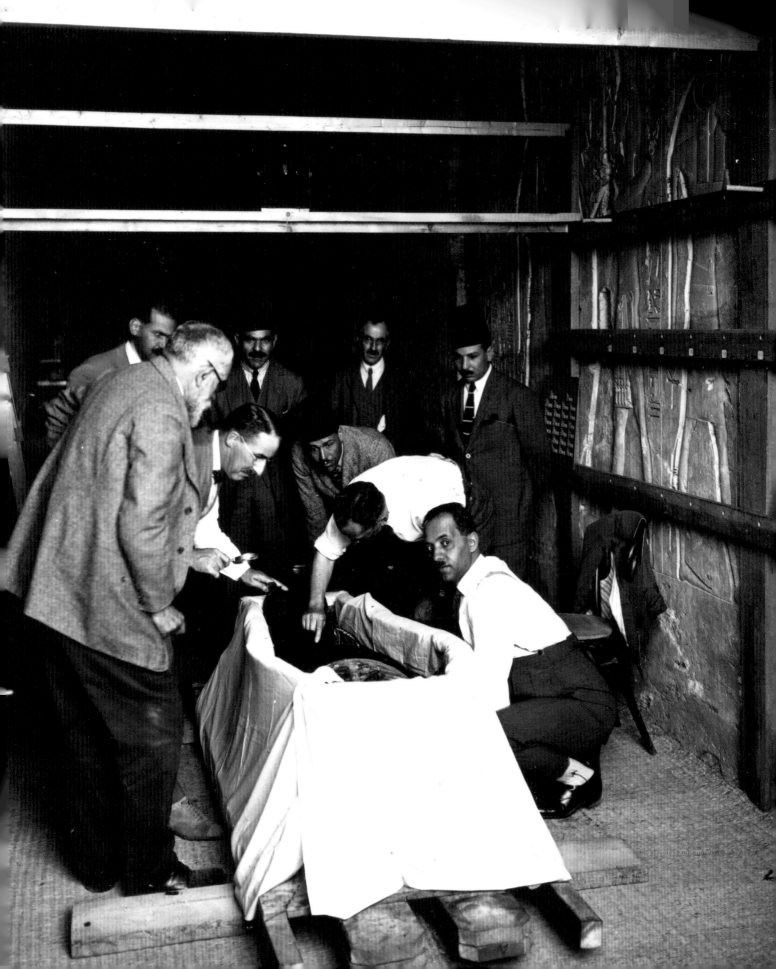

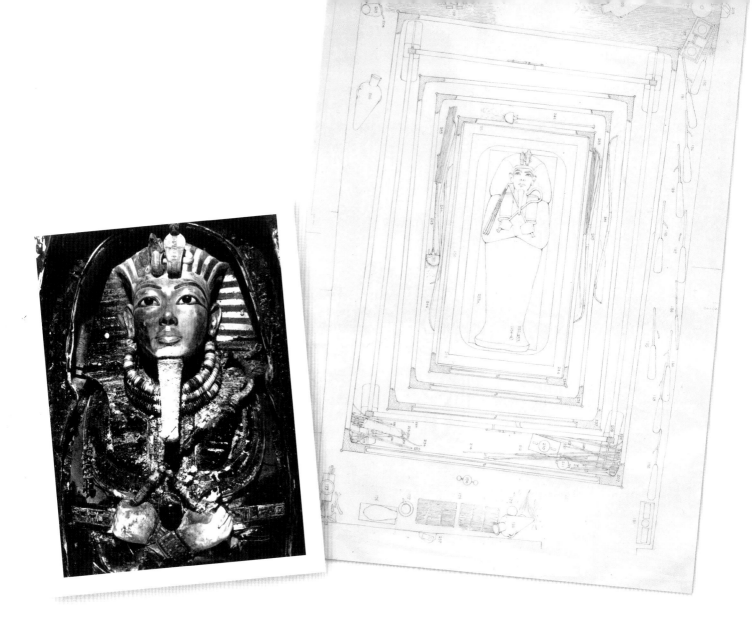

◐ Douglas Derry makes the initial incision in the outer wrappings of Tutankhamun's mummy.

◐ The King's funerary mask is revealed.

◐ Howard Carter's plan of the Burial Chamber containing a nest of shrines enclosing a stone sarcophagus and inner coffins.

radiographer whom Carter intended to X-ray the mummy in advance of any autopsy had died en route, and no other specialist was available.

The process of unwrapping and examining the mummy began on 11 November 1925 and was led by Carter, Douglas Derry, Professor of Anatomy of the Cairo Medical School, and Dr Seleh Bey Hamdi, former Director of the Medical School. It took place in the outer corridor of the tomb of Seti II, and was attended by Lucas, Burton, and various Egyptian and European dignitaries.

The brittle surface of the mummy was first coated in a layer of paraffin wax and the decayed wrappings were cut and removed in large pieces. These wrappings had been reduced to a soot-like consistency which Lucas explained as some kind of slow spontaneous combustion. All the king's limbs, fingers, and toes had been individually bandaged and the front of the body had been packed with sheets of linen. Some 150 amulets and other objects were recovered from within the mummy wrappings, the appearance and position of each of them carefully documented in drawings by Carter and photographs by Burton. Finally the body was revealed. The mask enclosing Tutankhamun's head had become stuck by the same consolidated unguents that covered the rest of the mummy. Hot knives were used to melt these resins so that the head and the mask could be removed. The blackened material had also to be chiselled away from beneath the body, which was dismantled to allow it to be separated from the coffin.

Following the autopsy, Derry concluded that Tutankhamun had been around 1.65 m (5 ft 5 in) tall in life and that he had died between the ages of 17 and 19. As ancient inscriptions indicated that the king had reigned for some nine years, this suggested that his accession to the throne must have occurred when he was a nine-year-old boy. Derry was unable to determine any possible causes of Tutankhamun's death; there were traces of numerous incisions on the king's body, but many of these 'injuries' may have resulted from the embalming process.

⊙ Tutankhamun's mummified head following the disassembling of the body during the autopsy.

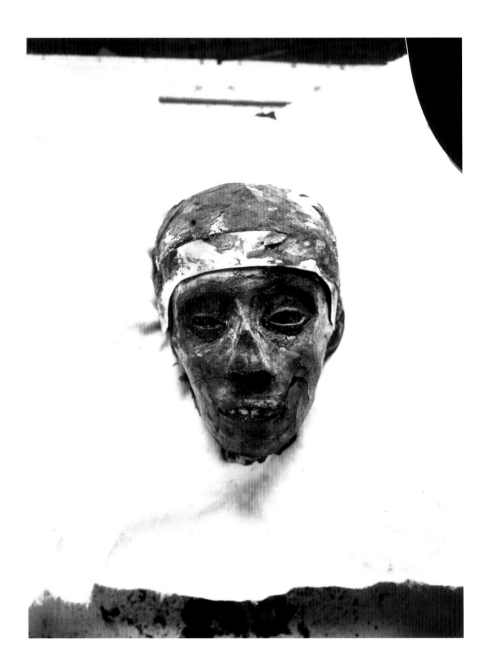

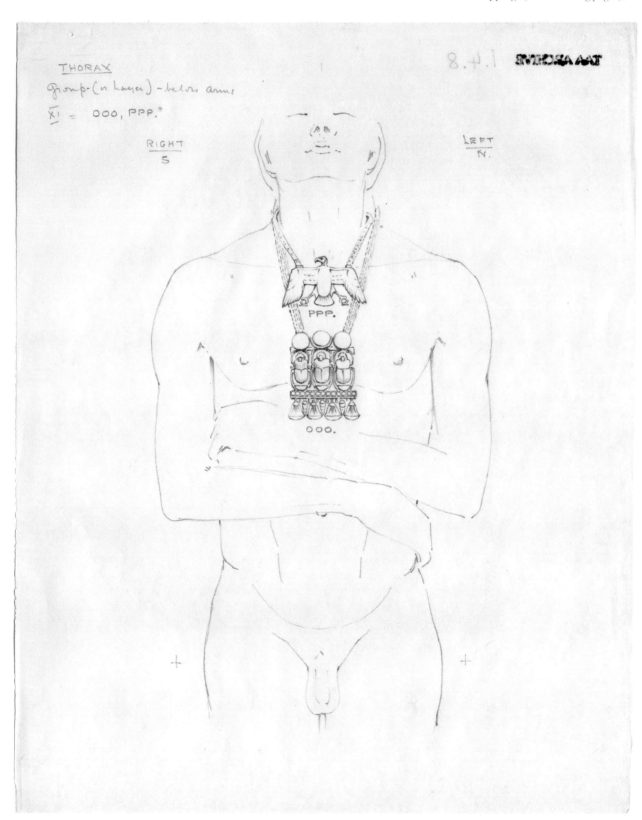

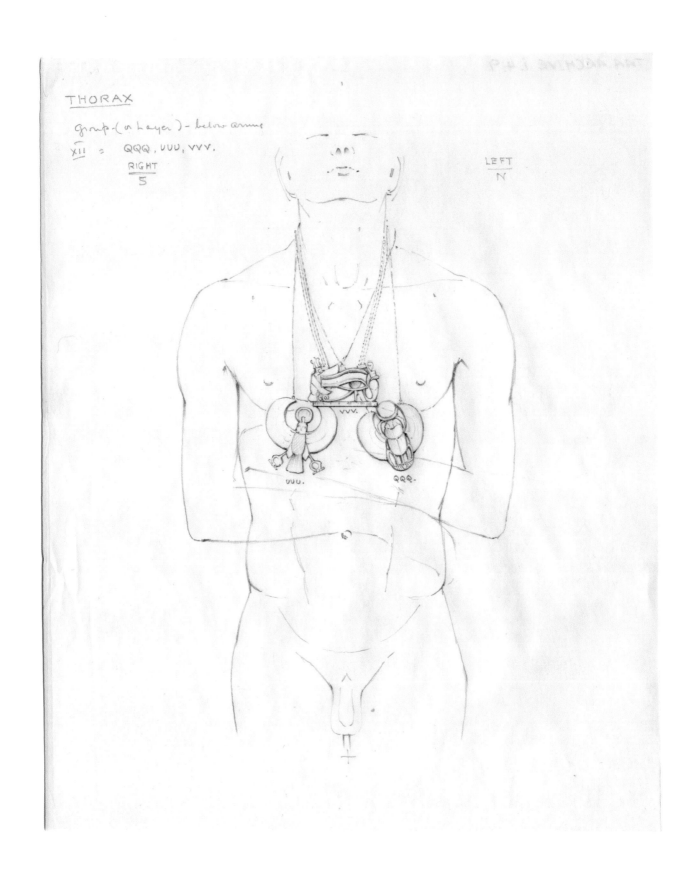

THORAX

Group - (or Layer) - below arms

XII = QQQ, UUU, VVV,

RIGHT
5

LEFT
N

UUU.

QQQ.

VVV.

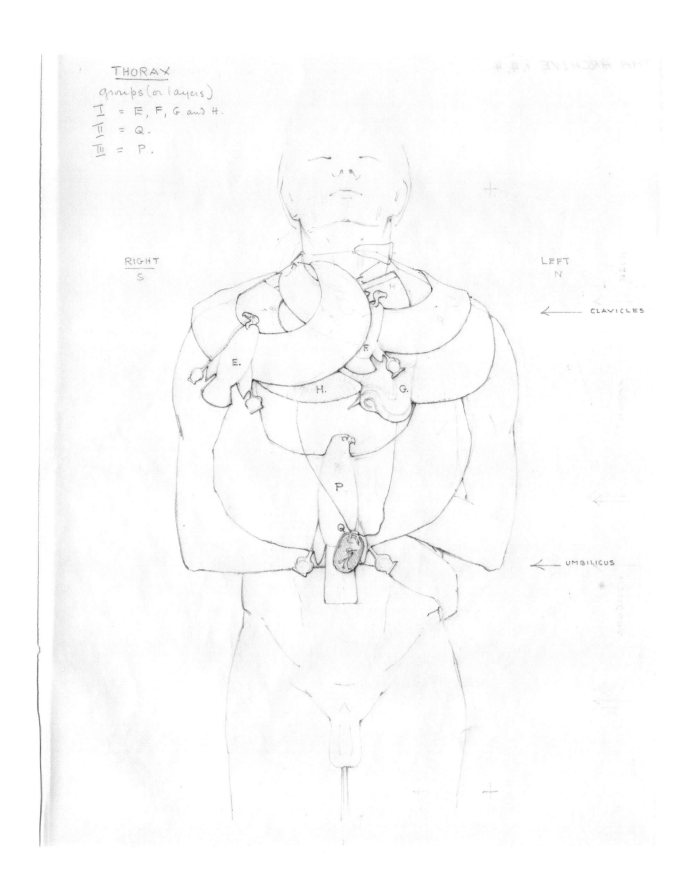

THORAX
groups (or layers)
I = E, F, G and H.
II = Q.
III = P.

RIGHT
S

LEFT
N

← CLAVICLES

← UMBILICUS

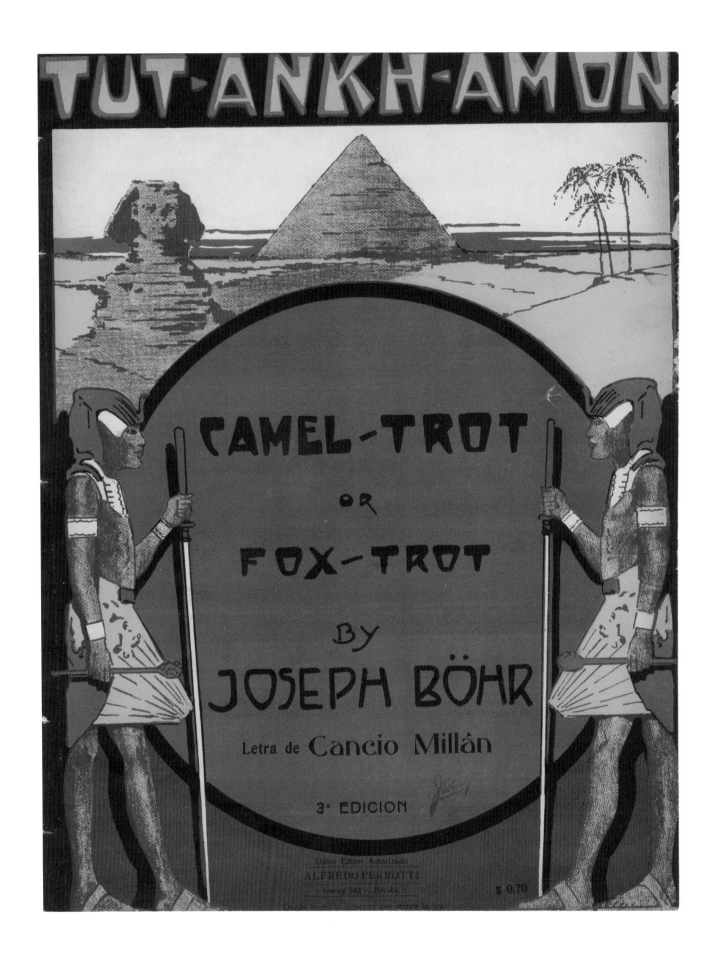

Tut-mania

'One cannot escape the name of Tut-Ankh-Amen anywhere.'

There is only one topic of conversation … One cannot escape the name of Tut-Ankh-Amen anywhere. It is shouted in the streets, whispered in the hotels, while the local shops advertise Tut-Ankh-Amen art, Tut-Ankh-Amen hats, Tut-Ankh-Amen curios, Tut-Ankh-Amen photographs, and tomorrow probably genuine Tut-Ankh-Amen antiquities. Every hotel in Luxor today had something a la Tut-Ankh-Amen … There is a Tut-Ankh-Amen dance tonight at which the piece is to be a Tut-Ankh-Amen rag.
New York Times, 18 February 1923

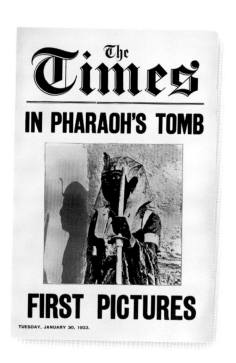

Although the first news reports of the discovery of the tomb were made in November 1922, it was not until the following year, particularly from February 1923 after the Burial Chamber was officially opened, that the international press began to take a greater interest in Tutankhamun. What helped especially to capture the attention of news reporters was a contract agreed between *The Times* in London and Lord Carnarvon. The newspaper paid £5,000 to Carnarvon for exclusive access to the tomb and a first look at its contents, with sole rights to supply the world's press with news and photographs; the first 'official' report was made on 30 January 1923. Today such a practical arrangement might be taken for granted, but for its time this media deal was extremely unusual – perhaps the first of its kind, in fact – and other newspapers, including the Egyptian press, reacted with indignation. Intense rivalry grew among reporters for access to stories and some of them became creative, developing accounts of the tomb's discovery that suggested secrecy and mystery.

As the number of press reports increased, Tutankhamun and his tomb rapidly captured the public imagination, especially in the United States. Technology – telegraph, telephone, and moving film – made it possible for stories to 'break' almost instantaneously as new finds were made. The *New York Times*, for example, cabled coverage of the discoveries almost daily.

Carter was only too aware of the developing hysteria that his discovery was generating between the press and the public. The number of visitors to the

Sheet music cover, 1924–26.

The cover of a special photographic supplement issued by *The Times*, 30 January 1923.

tomb increased enormously and, encouraged to travel to Egypt by companies such as Thomas Cook & Son and Cunard, thousands of people descended each year on the Valley of the Kings as the excavation progressed. Whenever Carter felt it was safe for particular objects to be exposed to sunlight and heat for a short time, they were moved from the tomb to the conservation laboratory on uncovered trays, much to the excitement of the waiting press and tourists. However, reporters were increasingly frustrated by Carter's meticulous and time-consuming methods for the clearance of the tomb and, driven by a demand for new images and 'angles', journalists hounded him and his team. This did little to placate Carter's famously irascible character.

Carter's lack of diplomatic finesse became a real issue within the context of the wider politics of Egypt. In 1919 a revolution against the British Protectorate occupation of the country had led to independence in 1922 and the establishment of a new constitution the following year. Egyptian nationalists, already angered at Lord Carnarvon's deal with *The Times*, resented the lack of local involvement in the recording and clearance of the tomb. As a matter of principle, Carter stubbornly refused to provide greater access. On 13 February 1924, after increasing tensions between the archaeologist, politicians, and the press, Carter stopped work and closed the tomb. The concession to excavate was cancelled by the Egyptian government and Carter travelled to the United States and Canada, where he gave numerous lectures about the discovery of Tutankhamun to packed lecture halls and theatres. It was not until 13 January 1925 that work in the tomb resumed – Carter's concession was restored, *The Times* lost its exclusive rights, and the Carnarvon estate gave up any claims to the contents of the tomb. It would be the Egyptian government who would finance the remaining seven seasons of work.

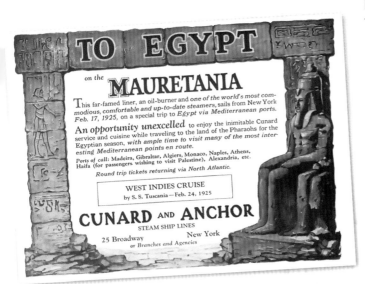

⬆ Advertisement for a steam ship cruise to Egypt, 1925.

➡ Lord Carnarvon accompanies Queen Elisabeth of the Belgians on a tour of Tutankhamun's tomb, 18 February 1923.

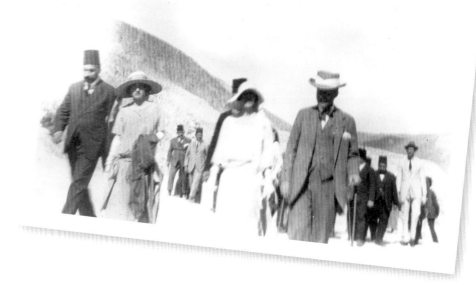

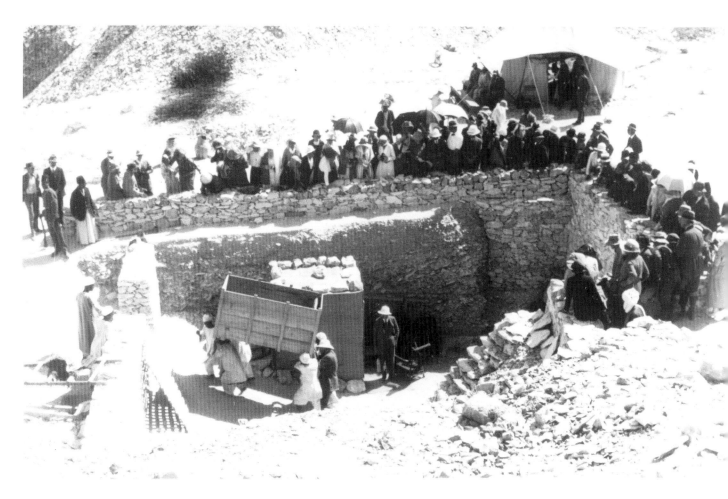

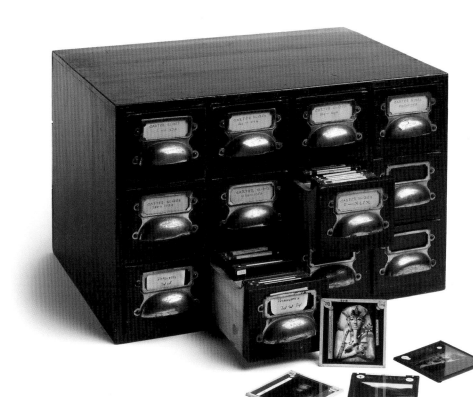

⬆ Tourists and journalists crowd around the tomb's entrance watching the removal of objects.

◀ Howard Carter's chest of glass lantern slides, including hand-tinted examples, used during his lecture tour of America.

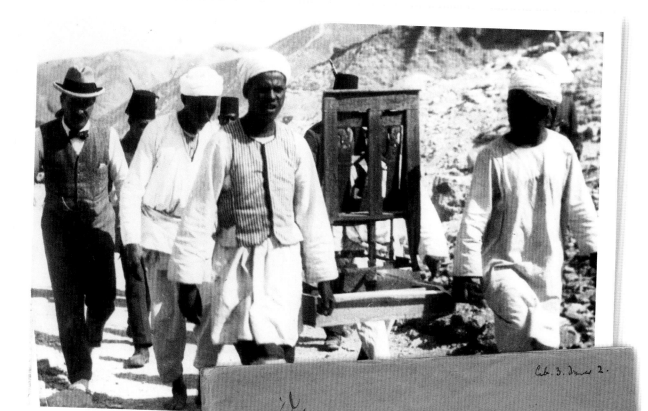

⬆ Howard Carter escorts one of Tutankhamun's thrones on its journey from the tomb to the conservation 'laboratory'.

➡ The 'Statement' issued by Howard Carter following the closure of the tomb in 1924.

Confidential

Cat. 3. Draw. 2.

The Tomb of Tut·ankh·amen

STATEMENT·

With Documents, as to the Events which occurred in Egypt in the Winter of 1923-24, leading to the ultimate break with the Egyptian Government

[*For Private Circulation only.*]

Cassell and Company, Limited
London, New York, Toronto and Melbourne

Tutankhamun, Tut–Ankh–Amen, 'King Tut'

When the outer door to the tomb was uncovered in 1922, the name in hieroglyphs stamped into the plaster was identified by Howard Carter as Tut-Ankh-**Amen**. As vowels are not indicated in ancient Egyptian scripts – they have been introduced by modern translators to help pronunciation – there are other possible vocalisations of the divine name that forms part of the royal name, such as the one preferred by many modern scholars: Tut-Ankh-**Amun** ('Living image of Amun'). In 1923, however, it was a shortened version of Tutankhamun that swept through popular culture. In some of his first letters home following the opening of the tomb, Lord Carnarvon made reference to 'King Tut', but it was in the United States that this form of the name took on a life of its own.

The song writer Harry Von Tilzer soon found he had scored a hit with *Old King Tut*, which was recorded by popular entertainers such as Jones and Hare and Sophie Tucker:

Three thousand years ago,
In history we know
King Tut-an-ka-men ruled a mighty land.
Mid laughter, song and tears,
He made a record that will always stand.

They opened up his tomb the other day and jumped with glee.
They learned a lot of ancient history:
His tomb instead of tears,
Was full of souvenirs.
He must have traveled greatly in his time.
The gold and silverware that they found hidden there,
Was from hotels of every land and clime.
While going through his royal robes they found up in his sleeve,
The first love letter Adam wrote to Eve.

◗ Bakelite record of 'Old King Tut' recorded by Billy Jones and Earnest Hare, 1923.

◗ Sheet music covers for American popular songs inspired by the discovery of Tutankhamun, 1923.

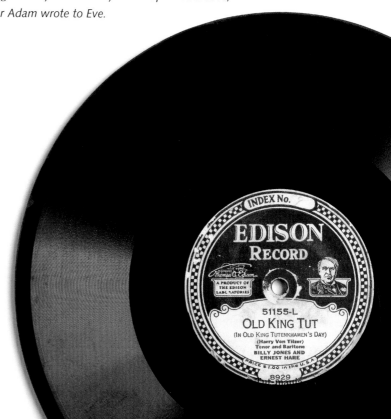

OLD KING TUT

WORDS BY
WILLIAM JEROME
MUSIC BY
HARRY VON TILZER

Harry Von Tilzer Music Pub. Co.
719 SEVENTH AVE   NEW YORK

MADE IN
USA

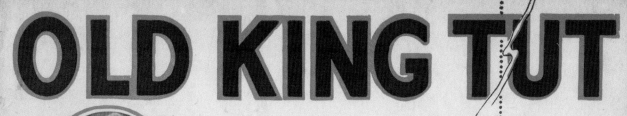

OLD KING TUT

WAS A WISE OLD NUT

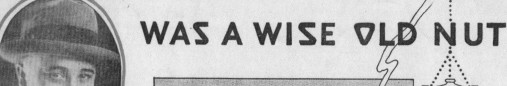

First Introduced by
LEO FITZPATRICK
*The Merry Old Chief of the Kansas
City Star's Nighthawk Radio Club*

Lyric by
Roger Lewis
Music by
Lucien Denni
writers of "Oceana Roll"

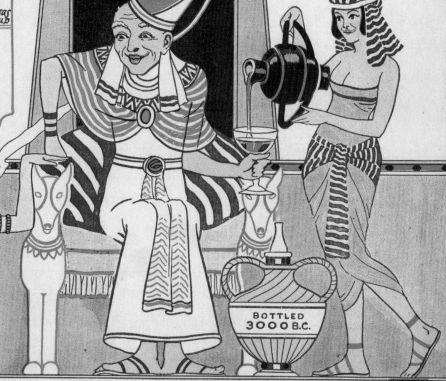

BOTTLED
3000 B.C.

HE GOT INTO HIS ROYAL BED
THREE THOUSAND YEARS B.C.
AND LEFT A CALL FOR TWELVE O'CLOCK
IN NINETEEN TWENTY THREE

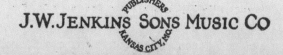

J.W. JENKINS SONS MUSIC CO
PUBLISHERS
KANSAS CITY, MO.

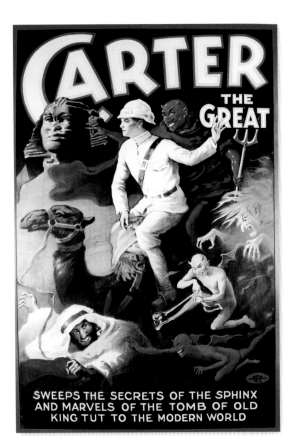

Poster of the stage magician
'Carter the Great', 1923.

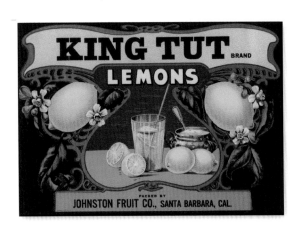

Advertising label from California,
1920s.

Songs and dance music inspired by Tutankhamun became the latest craze. Indeed, the success of *Old King Tut* spurred a competing music company to produce *Old King Tut Was a Wise Old Nut*. 'King Tut' became the name given to products, businesses, and even the pet dog of US President Herbert Hoover. The Tutankhamun 'brand' had mass popular appeal. Howard Carter also became part of the excitement, and was credited in some newspapers as being an American. Inspired by his namesake's discovery, the American stage magician Charles Carter (1874–1936), who was known as 'Carter the Great', proclaimed in his 1923 advertising poster: 'Carter the Great Sweeps the Secrets of the Sphinx and Marvels of the Tomb of Old King Tut to the Modern World'. It would be several years before the autopsy of Tutankhamun's mummy would reveal that King Tut had not been 'Old'.

Inspiring Contemporary Fashion

A fascination with royalty made it almost inevitable that the fashion world would look to Tutankhamun for inspiration, especially after Elisabeth, Queen of the Belgians, visited the tomb, pursued by the press. Dresses, coats, jackets, and accessories were soon being designed with Egyptian motifs or advertised as inspired by the riches found in the tomb.

Even modern hairstyles could be linked to ancient Egypt, according to a headline in the *Los Angeles Times*:

Ancient Egypt Lives Again in Hollywood: Even the Bobbed Hair Reincarnated From the Flappers Who Lived When Tombs Were Built

Ancient Egypt had been a popular theme in jewellery design since the early nineteenth century. With the discovery of the tomb, however, new models emerged. In a special Tutankhamun edition of 26 January 1924, the *Illustrated London News* assembled a series of 'archaeological' pieces from Cartier London. More frivolous items of jewellery were also available for a less well-heeled market.

'The decorative splendors of the Tut-ankh-amen period are reflected in the rich embroidery motif on this distinguished Wrap-Over Coat with its aristocratic collar of bisque squirrel.'

Clockwise from left: Green glass 'Tut Bowl', 1923; Royal Doulton jug, 1923–29; Carlton 'Tutankhamun' ware, 1924–27; Huntley and Palmers Egyptian biscuit tins, 1924.

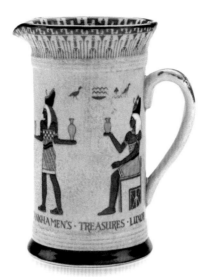

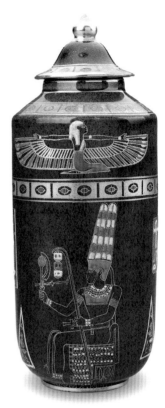

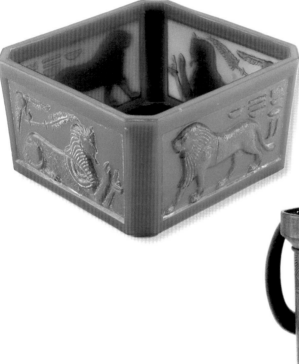

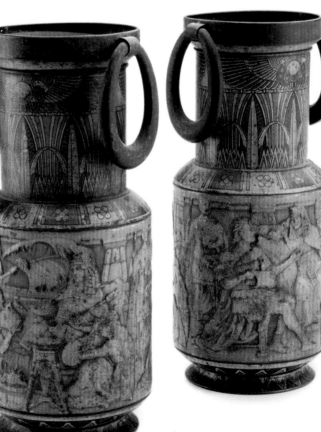

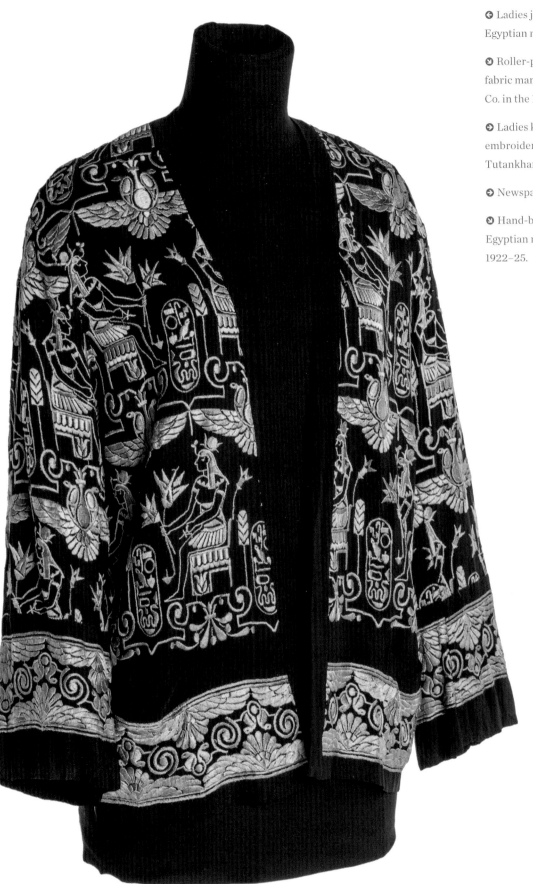

Ladies jacket embroidered with Egyptian motifs, about 1930.

❯ Roller-printed cotton furnishing fabric manufactured by F. Steiner & Co. in the 1920s.

❯ Ladies kid gloves, the wrists embroidered with the name of Tutankhamun in hieroglyphs, 1920s.

❯ Newspaper advertisements, 1923.

❯ Hand-beaded lurex jacket with Egyptian motifs, Paris, France, 1922–25.

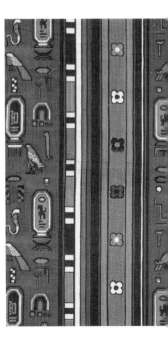

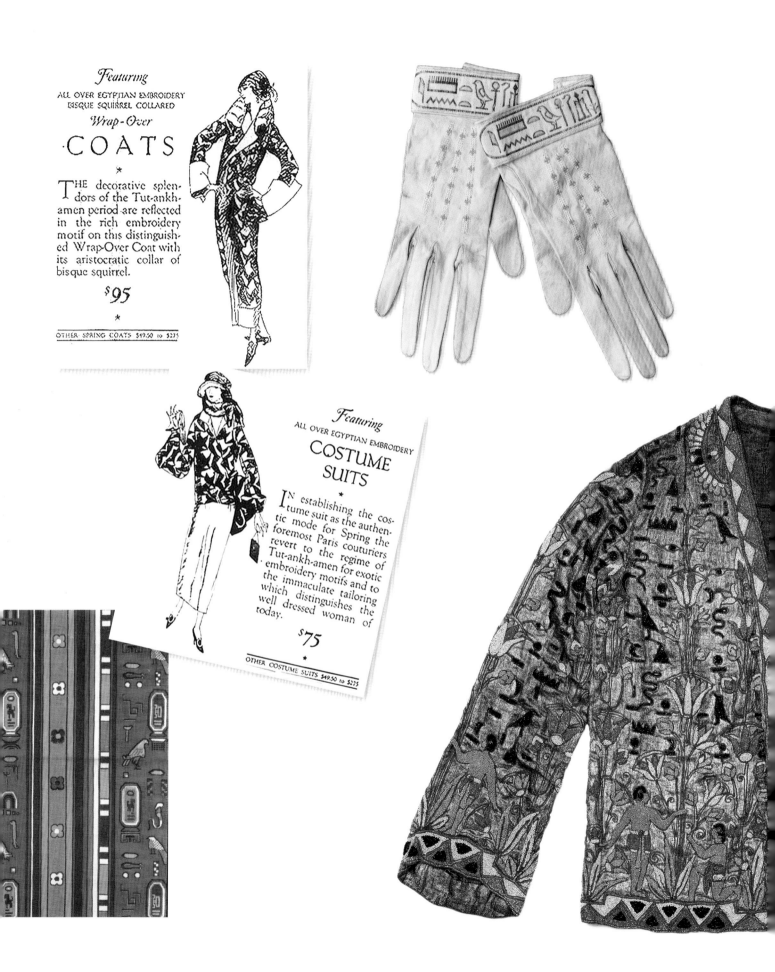

Featuring

ALL OVER EGYPTIAN EMBROIDERY
BISQUE SQUIRREL COLLARED

Wrap-Over

·COATS·

*

THE decorative splendors of the Tut-ankhamen period are reflected in the rich embroidery motif on this distinguished Wrap-Over Coat with its aristocratic collar of bisque squirrel.

$95

*

OTHER SPRING COATS $19.50 to $275

Featuring

ALL OVER EGYPTIAN EMBROIDERY

COSTUME SUITS

*

IN establishing the costume suit as the authentic mode for Spring the foremost Paris couturiers revert to the regime of Tut-ankh-amen for exotic embroidery motifs and to the immaculate tailoring which distinguishes the well dressed woman of today.

$75

*

OTHER COSTUME SUITS $49.50 to $275

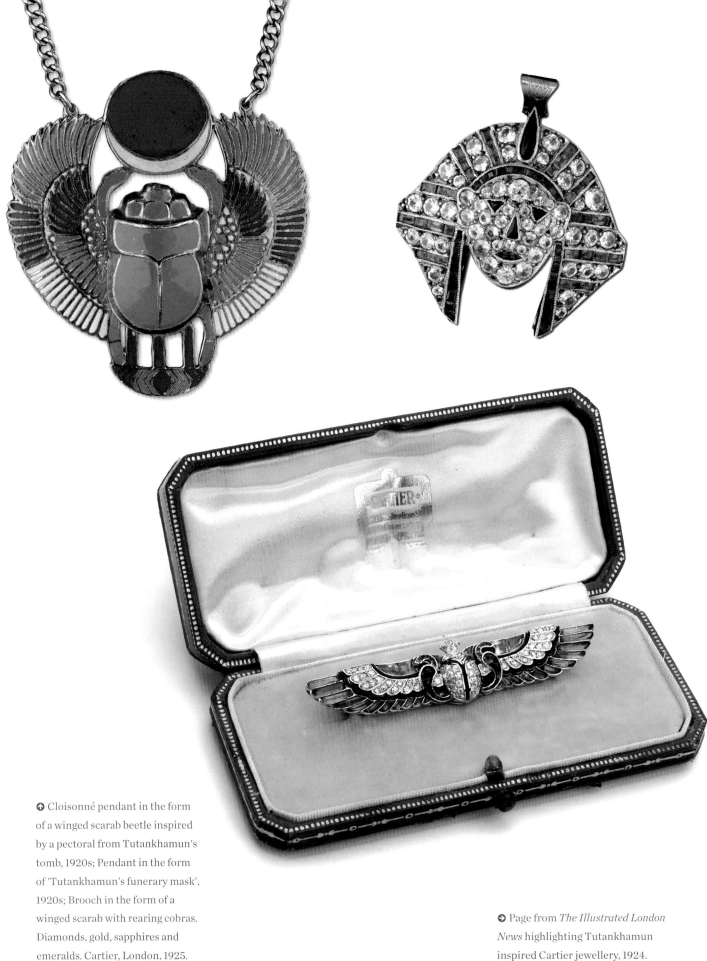

⬆ Cloisonné pendant in the form of a winged scarab beetle inspired by a pectoral from Tutankhamun's tomb, 1920s; Pendant in the form of 'Tutankhamun's funerary mask', 1920s; Brooch in the form of a winged scarab with rearing cobras. Diamonds, gold, sapphires and emeralds. Cartier, London, 1925.

➡ Page from *The Illustrated London News* highlighting Tutankhamun inspired Cartier jewellery, 1924.

THE "TUTANKHAMEN" INFLUENCE IN MODERN JEWELLERY.

REPRODUCED BY COURTESY OF CARTIER, LTD., 175, NEW BOND STREET, W.I.

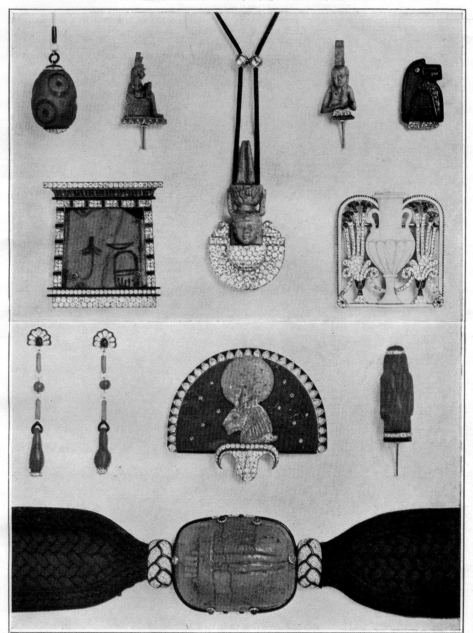

EGYPTIAN TRINKETS FROM 1500 TO 3000 YEARS OLD ADAPTED AS MODERN JEWELLERY: BROOCHES, PENDANTS, EARRINGS, AND HAT-PINS SET WITH REAL ANTIQUES; AND A TUTANKHAMEN REPLICA.

Women interested in Egyptology, who desire to be in the Tutankhamen fashion, can now wear real ancient gems in modern settings as personal ornaments. We illustrate here some typical examples, by courtesy of Cartier, the well-known Bond Street jewellers. Taken in order from left to right, beginning at the top, the objects are described as follows :— (1) A bead of glazed faience of the Twenty-second Dynasty (about 900 B.C.). Its deep colour shows its age. (2) A figure of Isis and child in glazed faience (Twenty-sixth Dynasty, 600 B.C.) set as a hat-pin. (3) A faience head of Isis (600 B.C.) set as a pendant. (4) A faience bust of Isis (600 B.C.) set as a hat-pin. (5) A glazed faience head of Hapi, the monkey-god of the Nile (Twenty-second Dynasty, 900 B.C.) set as a hat-pin. (6) A miniature temple in glazed faience (900 B.C.) set as a brooch. (7) This is the only object on the page which is not an actual Egyptian antique. It is a miniature replica of the most beautiful alabaster vase found in Tutankhamen's Tomb. (8) Ear-rings of lotus seeds and glazed faience tubes (Eighteenth Dynasty, 1500 B.C.) set with diamonds and onyx. (9) A sacred ram in glazed faience (600 B.C.) set as a brooch. (10) A figure of Ta-urt, protecting goddess of women, in sardonyx (Thirteenth Dynasty) set as a hat-pin. (11) A scarab (Twenty-first Dynasty, 1000 B.C.) set in coloured stones as a clasp for a twisted silk belt.

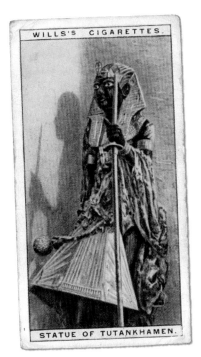

WILLS'S CIGARETTES.

STATUE OF TUTANKHAMEN.

The 'Guardian' Statues

The sealed entrance to Tutankhamun's Burial Chamber was flanked by two life-size, wooden, and gilded statues of the king holding a mace and staff. Harry Burton's photograph of the figure standing on the right, with a piece of ancient cloth still hanging over its left arm, was among the first to be published by *The Times*. Before the opening of the king's coffin and the discovery of the funerary mask, this statue became the most famous image of Tutankhamun and was reproduced on a wide range of products.

Replicas of the two 'guardians', as well as copies of other objects discovered in the Antechamber, were among the most popular exhibits of the British Empire Exhibition that took place at Wembley, Middlesex between 1924 and 1925. The replicas, made by the Hull sculptor William Aumonier and a team of assistants, were based on published photographs and advice from the Egyptologist Arthur Weigall. It took Aumonier some eight months to reproduce the objects, using gold leaf with an estimated value of £1,000.

Although only the Antechamber had been investigated by this date, the Exhibition brochure claimed ambitiously that the display was:

'A complete replica of the tomb of the Egyptian King recently discovered at Luxor, Egypt by Lord Carnarvon and Mr Howard Carter – entrance 1/3, children 8d.'

The creation of the replicas enraged Howard Carter. He assumed that they had been produced using photographs which were the property of the Carnarvon–Carter expedition and thus represented an infringement of copyright. Carter therefore instructed his solicitors to issue a writ against the Directors of the Exhibition. His case was challenged successfully and, while Carter toured the United States, the writ was withdrawn. After the Wembley exhibition closed, the replicas were purchased and donated to the people of Hull, where they are now on display in the Hands on History Museum.

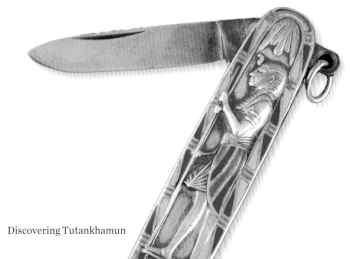

◈ Cigarette card with a 'guardian' statue, number 11 in the 'World of Wonders' series, 1926.

◈ Penknife decorated with an image of a 'guardian' statue, 1920s.

◈ Photograph by Harry Burton of one of the two 'guardian' statues as found in the Antechamber.

◈ Pages from *The Illustrated London News* featuring replicas made for the 'British Empire Exhibition,' 1924.

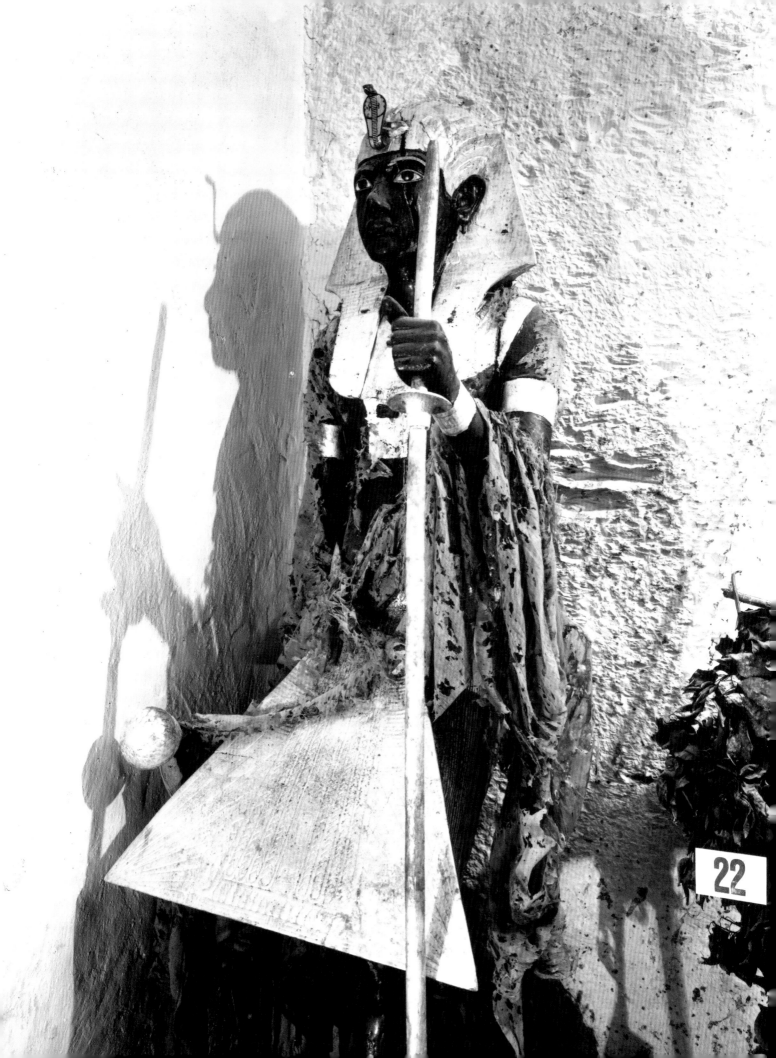

22

DOUBLY INTERESTING SINCE THE "STRIKE" AND "LOCK-OU"

PHOTOGRAPHS BY TO

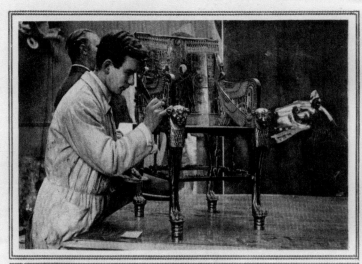

FOR "TUTANKHAMEN'S TOMB" AT WEMBLEY: MAKING AN EXACT MODEL OF THE GOLDEN THRONE, WITH ITS PAINTED PANEL.

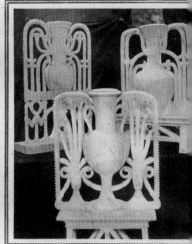

COPIED FROM THE EXQUISITE ALABASTER VASES FOU
IN THE TOMB: EXHIBITION REPLICAS.

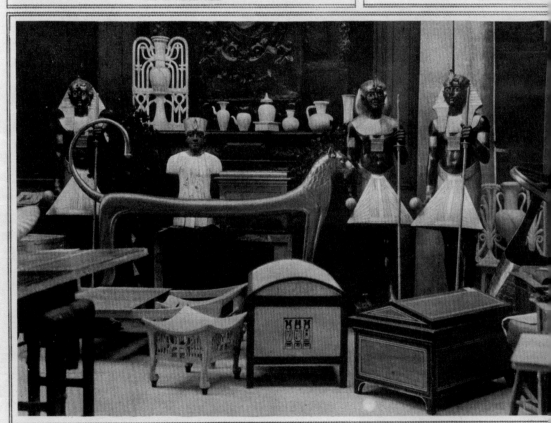

MODELS OF TUTANKHAMEN TREASURES MADE FOR THE REPLICA OF HIS TOMB IN THE EXHIBITION GROUNDS AT WEMBLEY: A LION COUCH, LIFE-SIZE STATUES OF THE KING, THE "MANNEQUIN" BUST, A FOOTSTOOL, VASES, BOXES, AND PART OF A ROYAL CHARIOT.

Since the deplorable events at Tutankhamen's tomb, where Mr. Howard Carter and his assistants recently ceased work and closed the tomb, as a pro against official "discourtesies" and "restrictions," and were subsequently themselves locked out by order of the Egyptian Government, it seems as though model of the tomb in the British Empire Exhibition grounds at Wembley must do duty for the real one as a place of pilgrimage for visitors. Admirable repl of the various objects found in the tomb have been constructed by Mr. William Aumonier, the architectural sculptor, in a carefully guarded room in Lond near Tottenham Court Road. The work is being done under the direction of a well-known Egyptologist, and it is claimed that it is accurate down to smallest detail. Our readers will be able to judge from the above photographs, compared with those of the actual objects which we have published f

T THE TOMB: TUTANKHAMEN REPLICAS FOR WEMBLEY.

G.P.U., AND I.B.

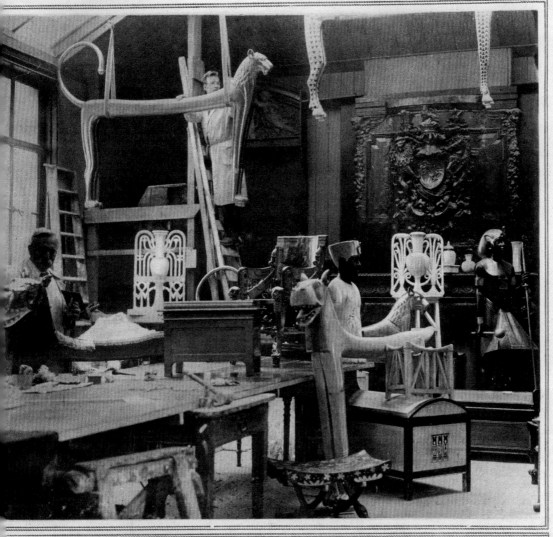

SHOWING THE TYPHONIC AND LION COUCHES AND THE (SPOTTED) LEGS OF THE HATHOR COUCH, THE GUARDIAN STATUES, THE THRONE, A FOOTSTOOL, VASES, SHRINES, AND PAINTED BOXES: MODELS MADE FOR "TUTANKHAMEN'S TOMB" IN THE BRITISH EMPIRE EXHIBITION AT WEMBLEY.

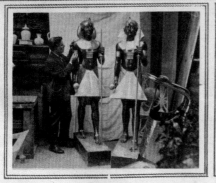

NKHAMEN
LICS IN
LICA: AT
K ON ONE
E CARVED
STATUES.

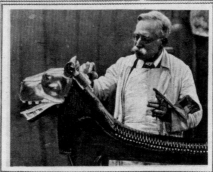

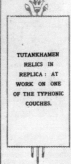

TUTANKHAMEN
RELICS IN
REPLICA: AT
WORK ON ONE
OF THE TYPHONIC
COUCHES.

to time, how closely the replicas correspond with their originals. Mr. Aumonier, who is assisted by his two sons, comes of a family of craftsmen, of
enot descent. His father was also an architectural sculptor, and his grandfather a worker in gold. He himself has lately been engaged on the new
e of the Carlton Club, and the new headquarters of the Westminster Bank in Threadneedle Street. He made some of the miniature cakes of soap for
ueen's Doll's House (recently illustrated in our pages), which, it will be remembered, is likewise to be on view in the Exhibition at Wembley. It is
sting to recall that, up to the present, the only documentary evidence as to the colour of the Tutankhamen treasures has been published in "The
ated London News," from the natural colour photographs taken specially for that purpose.

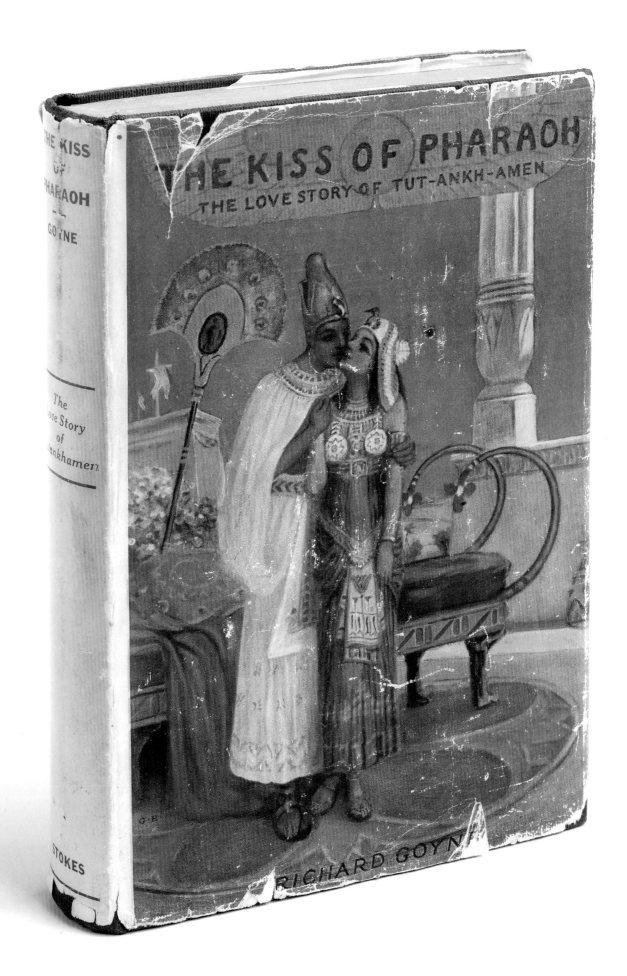

Tutankhamun in Fiction

1923 saw the publication of two 'Tutankhamun' novels which, given that they are romances, imagine the king as a young man.

Richard Goyne, a prolific writer of boxing and crime novels who also contributed stories to magazines for girls, wrote *The Kiss of Pharaoh: The Love Story of Tut-Ankh-Amen*. After many frustrations, the story sees the hero married to Rana (the name of Tutankhamun's real wife, Ankhesenamun, was not yet well known, and also something of a mouthful). Should the reader have missed the connection between the tale and the ongoing discoveries in Egypt, the book jacket makes it explicit:

> Those who have read of the finding and opening of Tutankhamen's luxuriously appointed tomb or who have seen newspaper pictures of the treasures will especially enjoy this novel of the young Pharaoh's brilliant reign and of his death, when all of Thebes stretched out across the desert in colorful procession to the magnificent tomb in the Valley of the Kings.
>
> It is a story of stirring adventure, and of love and hatred, picturing vividly those days of Old Egypt in which Tutankhamen reigned in all his glory and in a greater glory was laid away in the very tomb that Lord Carnarvon and Howard Carter entered three thousand years later, to bring forth its priceless treasures.

⬓ The Kiss of Pharaoh by Richard Goyne, 1923.

⬓ Frontispiece of King Tutankhamun: His Romantic History by Archie Bell, 1923.

The author Archie Bell attempted to give his novel *King Tut-Ankh-Amen: His Romantic History* a veneer of scholarship with an historical introduction and explanatory notes. Yet the title page reveals the book's synopsis:

'Relating how, as Prince of Hermonthis, he won the love of Senpa priestess of the temple of Karnak and through her interest achieved the throne of the Pharaohs.'

The Pharaoh's Curse

The notion that there might be dangers, both physical and supernatural, in opening the tomb were already evident in some of the first newspaper reports of the excavation. In December 1922 a *New York Times* correspondent visited the tomb and, in the course of describing the pair of life-size statues of Tutankhamun in the Antechamber, found an opportunity to include a sensationalist tale:

> *Each statue is crowned with a golden crown, bearing in front the royal serpent, or uraeus. As Thebes was the shrine of the cult of the serpent this is not unusual. Incidentally, the day the tomb was opened and the party found these golden serpents in the crowns of the two statues there was an interesting incident at Carter's house. He brought a canary with him this year to relieve his loneliness. When the party was dining that night there was a commotion outside on the veranda. The party rushed out and found a serpent of similar type to that in the crowns had grabbed the canary. They killed the serpent, but the canary died, probably from fright. The incident made an impression on the native staff, who regard it as a warning from the spirit of the departed King against further intrusion on the privacy of his tomb.*

An idea that the tomb might have been protected by poisonous booby-traps was suggested by the popular British author Marie Corelli. She claimed ownership of a rare book in which there is a warning that:

> *the most dire punishment follows any rash intruder into a sealed tomb. This book gives long and elaborate lists of the 'treasures' buried with several of the kings, and among these are named 'divers secret poisons enclosed in boxes such wise that they that touch them shall not know how they came to suffer'.*

Such warnings seemed justified when Lord Carnarvon became seriously ill. After his motorcar accident in 1901, Carnarvon had been left with a weak respiratory system and was prone to infections – it was for this reason that two years later he started spending his winters in Egypt's warm climate. In March 1923 a mosquito bite on his cheek was inadvertently reopened while he was shaving; blood poisoning set in, followed by pneumonia. On 5 April Lord Carnarvon died.

While *The Times* reported the earl's death in a sober manner, recalling his horseracing achievements as much as his contribution to Egyptology, many other newspapers recounted sensational accounts of ancient curses. The following appeared as a lead story in numerous US newspapers, including *The Telegraph-Herald*:

> *London, April 5. Ever since Carnarvon, the famous Egyptologist, rolled aside the stone protection of the tomb of Tutankhamen, thereby disturbing the pharaoh after a sleep of 3,500 years, he has been plagued by misfortune after misfortune. So believers in occultism of the orient have revived the ancient legend that an evil spell overtakes anyone who disturbs the tomb of pharaoh. They even wonder if the friends of Carnarvon, among them titled ladies of England and other countries who he has given beads and other relics from the death house of Tutankhamen will be similarly plagued.*

⊙ Report in the Australian *Sunday Times* of Lord Carnarvon's death and the curse of Tutankhamun, 20 May 1923.

To Prof Newberry

THE OLDEST AND THE NEWEST. FIRST AND FOREMOST, THE PUBLIC GOOD. 32 PAGES THREE PAPERS IN ONE

 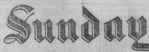 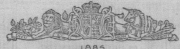

Sunday Times

1885

38th Year of Issue.

Subscription Rates:

Eight Page Coloured Comic Given Free with Every Copy of This Paper.

No. 1946. OFFICE: 100-101 CASTLEREAGH STREET. SYDNEY, N.S.W., AUSTRALIA, MAY 20, 1923. PRICE: THREEPENCE

Lord Carnarvon's Last Article

Specially written for the Sunday Times.

TREASURES FOR OUR MUSEUMS

AUSTRALIA for seven years will contribute to cost of excavations in Tut-ankh-Amen's home.

AUSTRALIA for seven years will receive pro rata share of relics so discovered.

Joining with Egypt Exploration Society, we are to Receive Full Share of Relics Found in Excavation Area Conceded to Late Lord Carnarvon

SEARCH FOR TUT-ANKH-AMEN RECORDS IN TEL-EL-AMARNA

The Sunday Times is able to announce that, through the offices of its Managing Director—Mr. Hugh D. McIntosh, M.L.C.—Australia is to assist in the researches of the Egypt Exploration Society, which is continuing the work of the late Earl of Carnarvon, discoverer of the tomb and mummy of Tut-ankh-Amen, a great Pharaoh of about 1400 B.C.

In return, the Egypt Exploration Society, during the currency of the subscription, is to allot to Australian museums, nominated by Mr. McIntosh, a "pro rata" amount of any relics discovered by the Society.

Before his death, Lord Carnarvon had secured from the Egyptian Government concession to dig at Tel El Amarna, the locality from which Tut-ankh-Amen came to Thebes; and had transferred his claim to the Exploration Society. Very valuable discoveries are expected in this region; and there is no doubt that Australian museums will benefit richly from the agreement.

In the article below, which Lord Carnarvon sent to Mr. McIntosh while suffering from the illness of which he died, Lord Carnarvon describes his "dig" at Tut-ankh-Amen's tomb and his hopes from the site at Tel El Amarna. A further special interest attaches to the article in that it was the last to be written by Lord Carnarvon before his melancholy and mysterious death.

"NO MORE INTERESTING PERIOD CAN BE FOUND IN EGYPTIAN HISTORY"

Why Funds Are Wanted, and What Results Lord Carnarvon Expected

AUSTRALIA AND EGYPT

Sir John Maxwell Recalls Deeds in War, and Welcomes Our Aid in Archaeology

DETAILS OF THE AGREEMENT

Branch of Egypt Exploration Society To Be Formed in Australia

"THE CURSE OF OSIRIS"

Superstitions Legend Round Lord Carnarvon's Death

MARIE CORELLI'S POISON THEORY

Conan Doyle Puts Suspicion on Tut-ankh-Amen

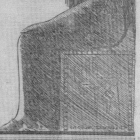

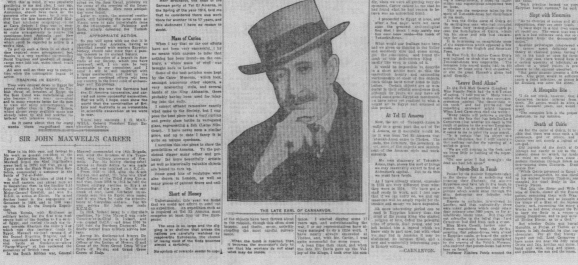

THE LATE EARL OF CARNARVON.

—CARNARVON.

SIR JOHN MAXWELL'S CAREER

Tut-mania 83

Among the most prominent recipients of Tutankhamen gifts from Lord Carnarvon are the queen of the Belgians and Lady Elizabeth Bowes-Lyon, who is to become the bride of the Duke of York.

When the ancient kings of Egypt were buried it has been recorded the priests said prayers imploring the wrath of the devils to descend upon anyone despoiling the tomb of a pharaoh.

Celebrity backing for the idea of a curse came from Sir Arthur Conan Doyle, author of the Sherlock Holmes stories and a noted spiritualist:

New York, April 5. Sir Arthur Conan Doyle, who arrived in this country yesterday for a second series of lectures on spiritualism, today expressed belief "that an evil elemental" brought into being by Egyptian occultism or the spirit of Tutankhamun might have caused the death of Lord Carnarvon.

Others were more sceptical:

THE DETROIT NEWS. Chicago, April 6. Prof. D.D. Luckenbill, Egyptologist at the University of Chicago and assistant to Prof. James Henry Breasted, who accompanied the Carnarvon expedition, characterised as "pure bosh" published stories on the curse theory of Lord Carnarvon's death. "An Egyptian king wasn't worried about what men were going to do long after his death," he said. "He decorated his grave and ordered luxurious trappings to be buried with him so that these articles might placate the 42 gods whose approval he must win before his soul might find peace. His interests were purely spiritual," said Prof. Luckenbill. Most of the inscriptions found in Egyptian tombs were biographical, he said, explaining that Babylonian inscriptions often were found to bear imprecations upon future molesters.

Academic accuracy aside, the press soon reported a false story that a written curse had been found in the king's tomb – *Death shall come on swift wings to him who toucheth the tomb of Pharaoh.* Carter even received letters from concerned members of the public containing advice on how best to counter the pharaoh's curse.

The Pharaoh's Curse and Hollywood

Inspired by reports of Tutankhamun's curse, the Hollywood producer Carl Laemmle Jr, who had achieved great success with his films *Dracula* and *Frankenstein*, looked to develop another horror film. A screenplay called *Cagliostro* was rewritten and titled *Im-Ho-Tep*, only becoming *The Mummy* just before it was released in 1932, with the lead played by Boris Karloff:

It is 1921 and an archaeological expedition to Egypt discovers the mummy of Im-ho-tep, a prince who had been buried alive for sacrilege. In the tomb is also found the Scroll of Thoth which can bring the dead back to life. A young archaeologist reads aloud the Scroll and revives Im-ho-tep. Ten years later, disguised as a modern Egyptian, Im-ho-tep attempts to reunite with his lost love Anck-es-en-Amon.

From horror, the Curse of the Mummy developed into slapstick comedy. In the 1939 film *We Want Our Mummy*, *The Three Stooges* explore the tomb of a certain King Rutentuten and his queen, Hotsy Totsy.

⊙ Cinema poster advertising *The Mummy*, starring Boris Karloff, 1932.

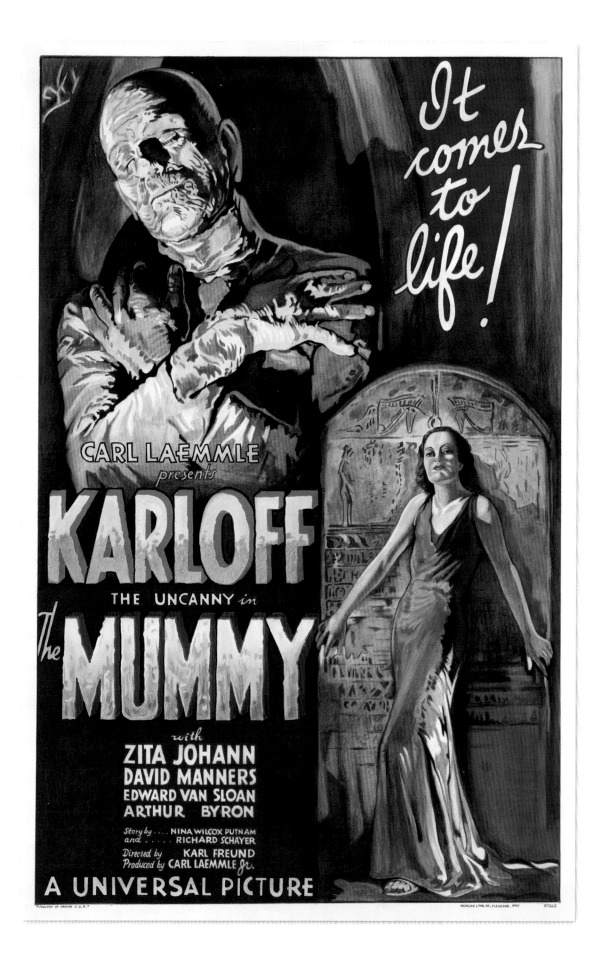

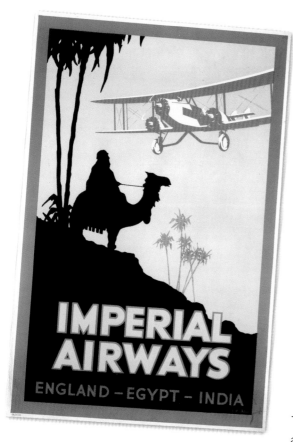

Tourism and Tours

Nothing could rival seeing the 'real' Tutankhamun, and tourism to Egypt grew dramatically as a result. In the early twentieth century international travel was largely the privilege of the rich. There were really only two options for travel to North Africa available in 1923: to go overland across Europe by car or train before taking a steamer through the Mediterranean Sea, or to make the entire journey by sea (a two-week voyage from London). Arriving at Alexandria or Port Said, tourists could take a trip to Cairo and see the sights of the capital city, its great museum and, especially, the pyramids at Giza, before boarding a steamer to visit the ancient sites along the River Nile. By the end of the decade, however, it had become possible to fly to Alexandria on a route established by Imperial Airways from Britain (Croydon) to India (Karachi, now in Pakistan).

By the 1960s safer and cheaper air transport allowed mass tourism to develop, and with it the possibility of bringing Tutankhamun to the world in a series of international museum 'blockbuster' exhibitions. Between 1961 and 1967 the first overseas exhibition of a number of artefacts from Tutankhamun's tomb travelled to 18 cities in the United States and six in Canada before also visiting Japan and France. It was, however, the exhibition *The Treasures of Tutankhamun* that began a second wave of Tut-mania. With the king's funerary mask as its star attraction, the show was launched at the British Museum on 30 March 1972. Opened by Queen Elizabeth II, more than 1.6 million visitors saw the exhibition, many queuing for hours around the forecourt of the museum. The collection of objects then moved on to other countries, including the USA, USSR, Japan, France, Canada, and West Germany. *The Metropolitan Museum of Art* organised the tour throughout the United States, where it was seen by more than eight million people. As with the mania of the 1920s, many people took the opportunity to exploit the 'King Tut' brand; in 1978, for example, the king was commemorated in song by the comedian Steve Martin and his band, the 'Tut Uncommons'.

↑ Poster advertising *Imperial Airways*, 1930s.

↓ Commemorative cover for the *Treasures of Tutankhamun* exhibition at the British Museum, 1972.

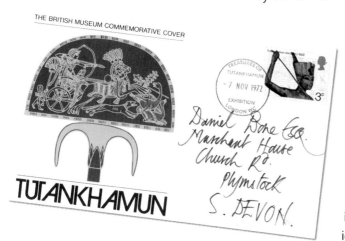

The Death of Tutankhamun

In 1968 Professor R G Harrison of the University of Liverpool took X-rays of Tutankhamun's body. The results fuelled another aspect of Tut-mania that still rages today – discussions about the possible causes of the king's death, ranging from accident or murder to long-term illness. In 2005 the first examination of the mummy by computer tomography (CT scan) was carried out, making it possible to eliminate many of the earlier theories. A break in the area above the king's left knee joint was, however, identified, and this could have led to complications that in

Tutankhamun's time would have meant certain death. Overall, however, the mummy had many broken bones and injuries, and these could have been the result of the embalming process as much as damage resulting from the unwrapping, dismantling during the autopsy or later treatment of the body.

More recently DNA analysis conducted in 2010 showed the presence of malaria in Tutankhamun's system, leading to a suggestion that the combination of two conditions (malaria and leiomyoma) may have led to his death. Alternative theories include that put forward in a television program aired on the US channel PBS entitled 'Ultimate Tut'. In this program computer simulations and physical tests were used to conclude that Tutankhamun had died after being hit by a chariot travelling at full speed.

◆ X-ray of the skull of Tutankhamun, 1968.

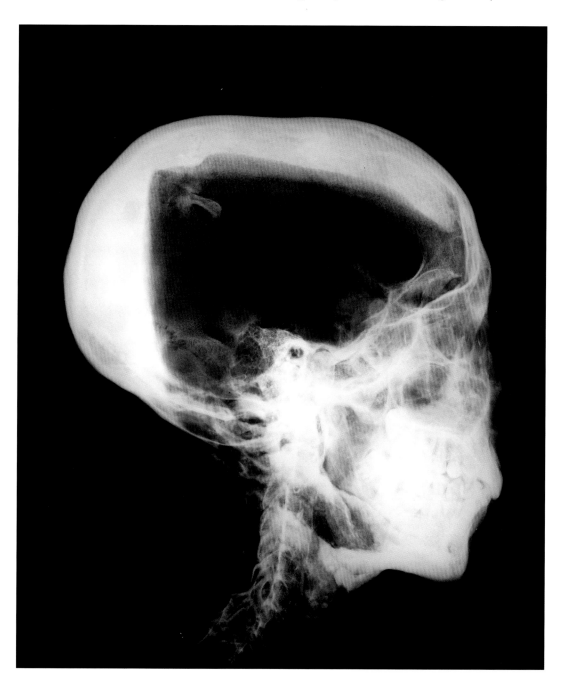

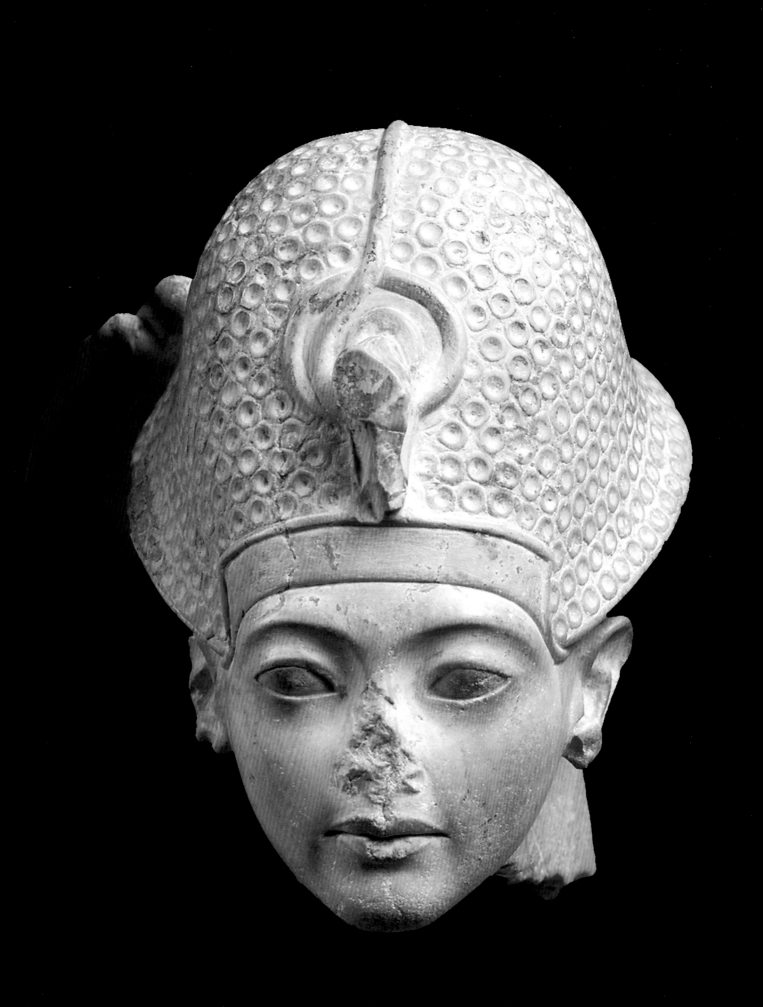

Re-evaluating Tutankhamun

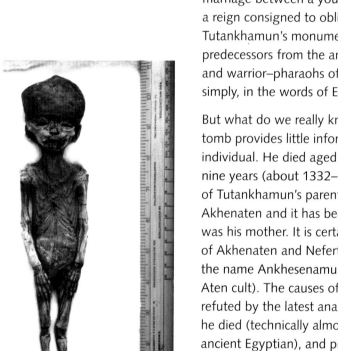

The contrast between Tutankhamun's modern fame and his insignificance in history has often been stressed. The popular image of Tutankhamun is that of a vulnerable young boy, perhaps suffering from ill-health, under the control of powerful court advisors who, taking advantage of the king's weakness, restored the old priestly establishment to power, thus ending King Akhenaten's experiment in monotheism; of a touchingly loving marriage between a young couple cut tragically short by death; and of a reign consigned to oblivion by conspiratorial successors, who usurped Tutankhamun's monuments and erased the names of his immediate predecessors from the annals of history. Compared with the pyramid builders and warrior–pharaohs of ancient Egypt's illustrious past, Tutankhamun is simply, in the words of Egyptologist Dr Zahi Hawass, 'the golden boy'.

But what do we really know about Tutankhamun? The content of his tomb provides little information to help illuminate Tutankhamun as an individual. He died aged around 18 years of age, having reigned for nine years (about 1332–1322 BC). Debates continue about the identity of Tutankhamun's parents, although it is possible that he was a son of Akhenaten and it has been suggested that Kiya, a lesser wife of Akhenaten, was his mother. It is certain that Tutankhamun's wife was a daughter of Akhenaten and Nefertiti called Ankhesenpaaten (she would adopt the name Ankhesenamun following her husband's abandonment of the Aten cult). The causes of his death are also hotly debated, each theory refuted by the latest analysis, but Tutankhamun was a grown man when he died (technically almost middle-aged in the average lifespan of an ancient Egyptian), and probably the father of the two children identified as female and found in individual coffins within the Treasury. Only one of Tutankhamun's daughters had reached full gestation, but she had died at or shortly after birth, leaving the king without a natural heir.

⊙ Indurated limestone head of Tutankhamun from a statue representing the king protected by the god Amun.

⊙ The foetus of one of Tutankhamun's daughters found in the Treasury.

The images of Tutankhamun found in his tomb have helped to promote ideas of a vulnerable 'boy king', as have some of the objects connected with his daily life, including several small ('child-sized') chairs and stools found among the tomb's contents. Perhaps the most touching scene appears on the backrest of the so-called 'Golden Throne'. Here Ankhesenamun is shown anointing her husband with perfume under the rays of the Aten. The design is in the 'Amarna style' that had emerged under King Akhenaten and embodies significant developments in the way in which Egypt's rulers were represented.

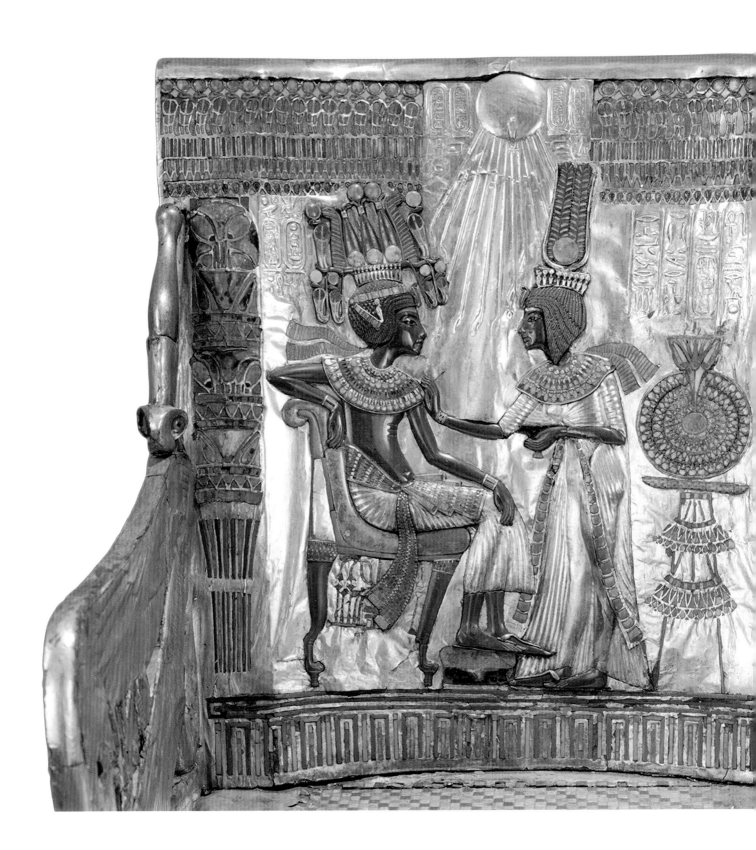

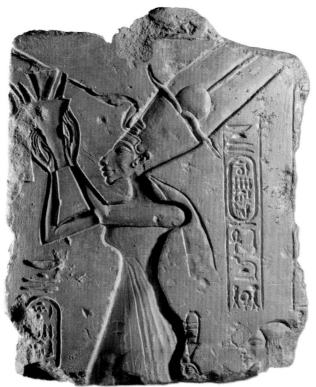

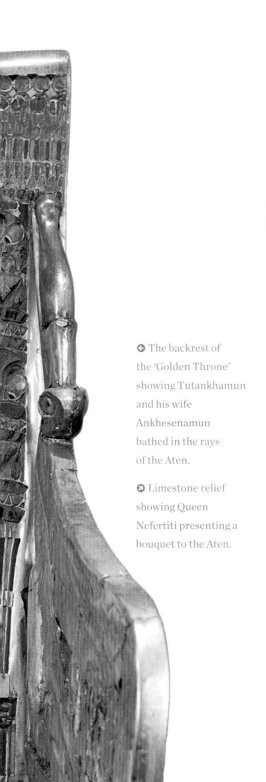

The backrest of the 'Golden Throne' showing Tutankhamun and his wife Ankhesenamun bathed in the rays of the Aten.

Limestone relief showing Queen Nefertiti presenting a bouquet to the Aten.

The ideology of the Aten religion focused on the divine royal family as a source of creation and perfection. The famous painted bust of Queen Nefertiti discovered at Tell el-Amarna encapsulates this concept, the regularity of her features extended and emphasised to stress a powerful presence and beauty. We probably should not read too many modern romantic notions into such aesthetically appealing images. Indeed, the Painted Box from the tomb, as well as reliefs in the temples of Luxor and Karnak, remind us that Tutankhamun could also be represented trampling prisoners of war under his feet and slaying enemies in battle, just like any traditional Egyptian ruler.

The small size and irregular plan of Tutankhamun's tomb suggest that it was intended for a non-royal burial. Perhaps the tomb was simply the only one available when the king died unexpectedly; the walls of the burial chamber were then decorated with appropriate imagery. It is possible, however, that this small tomb was being constructed for Ay, the king's vizier, who legitimised himself as the new pharaoh by burying Tutankhamun there; Ay is depicted on the tomb walls performing the funerary rites over the king's mummified body. Several years later, Ay would be buried in a large tomb in the West Valley, one perhaps originally intended for his predecessor. Of the objects buried with Tutankhamun, many had belonged to him in life and include items from when he was a boy, while others had been made for his predecessors or specifically for the tomb. This range of material of different dates might suggest that they had been gathered in some haste. However, in the absence of comparable royal tombs with their contents found intact, it is impossible to judge whether the objects selected to join Tutankhamun were unusual or typical of such burials.

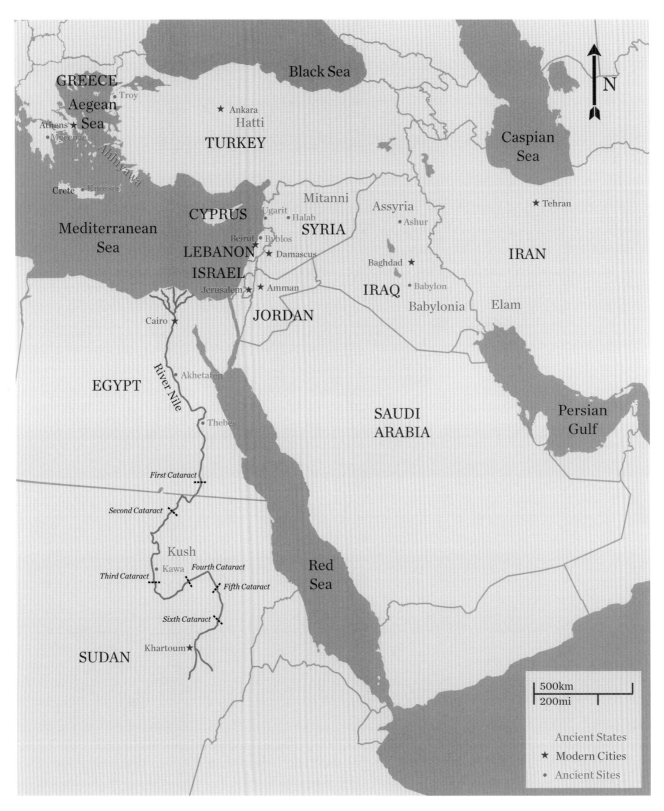

⬆ Map of ancient Egypt and the
wider Near East.

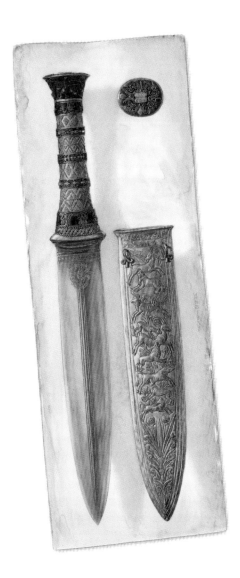

An International Age

While the contents of Tutankhamun's tomb shed little light on the man himself, they do help to illuminate the world in which he lived. The New Kingdom was a period of immense wealth and prosperity, a time in which Egypt's ruling elite enjoyed an opulent lifestyle provided by the exotic resources at the empire's disposal. It was also a period of intense international relations. By the time of Tutankhamun's birth, Egypt directly controlled territory reaching along the Nile Valley into central Africa and through the states of the eastern Mediterranean. Tribute, booty, and taxes flowed to the royal treasury where they were invested in monumental temple buildings, royal tombs, and funerary cults. Indeed, the country amassed vast quantities of materials from the Near East. As highlighted in the Amarna letters, gifts of exotic stones, metals, animals, and people were exchanged between the great powers of the day: Mitanni, Babylonia, Assyria, Ahhiyawa, and Hatti. The result was often a fusion of artistic styles.

Tutankhamun's tomb is especially rich in such 'international' imagery with, for example, hunting scenes – well-known from objects manufactured across the Near East – depicted on weapons, chariots, and wooden chests. Among them is the sheath of a gold dagger, with imagery that emphasises the traditional association of the pharaoh with the power of lions. The workmanship on the handle and sheath, with cloisonné feather-work, suggests that it was produced in an Egyptian workshop. However, the triangles of granulation on the hilt and the animal combat scenes on the sheath, which combine forms of movement known from both Aegean and east Mediterranean art, create a truly intercultural object.

'Now when His Majesty arose as king, the temples and estates of the gods and goddesses, from Elephantine to the Delta marshes, had fallen into ruin.'

⬆ Gouache painting on ivory by Winifred Brunton of a gold dagger and sheath from Tutankhamun's tomb, 1937.

The Obliteration of Tutankhamun

In his so-called 'Restoration Stela', found in the temple at Karnak, Tutankhamun presents himself as the restorer of order after the reign of Akhenaten, represented as a period of disorder and decline:

> Now when His Majesty [Tutankhamun] arose as king, the temples and estates of the gods and goddesses, from Elephantine to the Delta marshes, had fallen into ruin … The land was in confusion and the gods had turned their backs on this land … Hearts were faint in bodies because everything that had once been was destroyed.

The hieroglyphic inscription signals the abandonment of the Aten cult with a return to the traditional worship of the god Amun and the state pantheon. It records how Tutankhamun restored 'everything that was ruined, to be a monument for ever and ever', ordering the creation of new cult images of the old gods, 'rebuilding their sanctuaries' and 'endowing them with offerings for ever'.

Under Tutankhamun statues were erected depicting Amun in the image of the new king. The theme of royal restoration after a period of chaos is known from earlier Egyptian history as well as myth, and this powerful concept was appropriated by Tutankhamun's immediate successors. Following a brief rule of four years, Ay was succeeded by Horemheb, who had served as Tutankhamun's deputy, senior administrator, and commander of the army. Horemheb usurped numerous monuments of Tutankhamun, including the Restoration Stela. The tomb of Ay was defaced and the dismantling of the Aten temples at Karnak began alongside that of the city of Akhetaten. In this way Horemheb presented himself to future rulers of Egypt as the true restorer of order and rightful heir to the throne. Tutankhamun was consigned to the perceived chaos of the Amarna period and thus lost to history – at least until 1922!

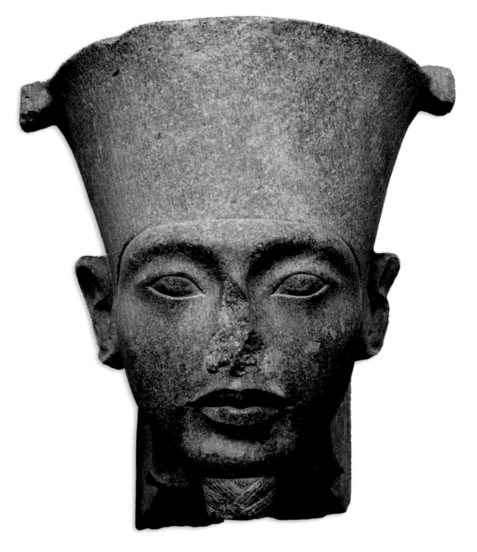

⊘ Head from a granodiorite statue of the god Amun with features resembling those of Tutankhamun.

⊙ Granite statue of Tutankhamun as a priest of the Nile god Hapy, usurped by Horemheb and inscribed with his name.

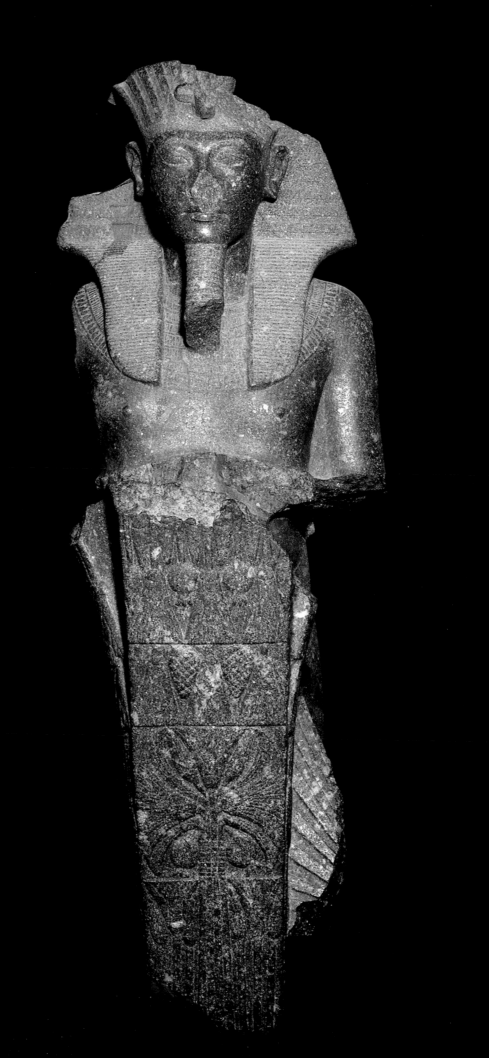

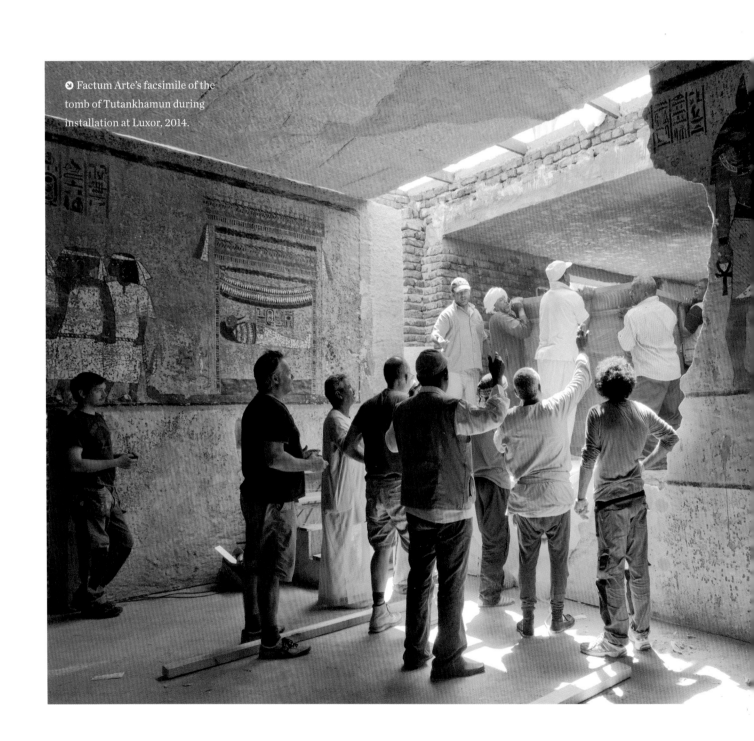

Factum Arte's facsimile of the tomb of Tutankhamun during installation at Luxor, 2014.

The Griffith Institute and the Future of Tutankhamun

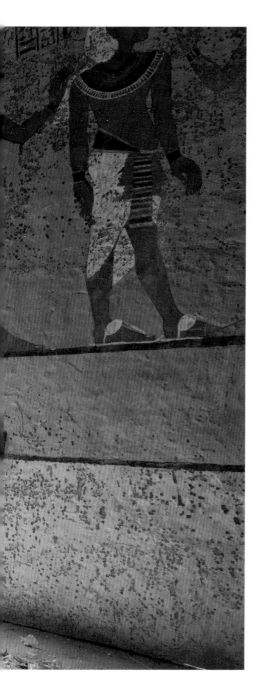

Preserving the Tomb and its Contents

Various projects have, in recent years, sought to ensure the preservation of Tutankhamun's tomb and an understanding of its contents for future generations. They have all been dependant on the Carter Archive in the Griffith Institute at Oxford.

Factum Arte. Prior to Egypt's recent political revolution in 2011 and a fall in the annual number of foreign tourists, the tomb of Tutankhamun was one of the most popular destinations for visitors to the Valley of the Kings – and no doubt it will be again in the future. On a busy day it would be viewed by approximately 1,000 people. This had a dramatic effect on the temperature, humidity, and dust in the small space which resulted in a deterioration of the structure of the walls, particularly the painted Burial Chamber. Previous restoration and consolidation treatments appear to have added to the problems.

The Factum Foundation has used the latest in digital technology to record the surface and structure of the interior of the tomb in astonishing detail. This has made it possible for them to produce an accurate facsimile that can be visited at Luxor, thus relieving pressure on the actual tomb. Working under the auspices of the Egyptian Supreme Council of Antiquities, the recording of the tomb was carried out in 2009 without interrupting the normal flow of visitors. Drawing on the records in the Carter Archive, comparisons could be made between current conditions and those revealed in 1922. As a result, missing fragments of painting from the south wall could be restored in the modern facsimile.

Tutankhamun: His Tomb and His Treasures **Exhibition.** In the future it is likely that only a few of the objects from Tutankhamun's tomb will be permitted to leave Egypt – the famous gold funerary mask, for example, is among those considered too vulnerable ever to leave the country again. Carefully made replicas allow for a reconstruction of parts of the tomb just as Lord Carnarvon and Howard Carter saw it. Using the Carter Archive, it was possible to reproduce all the objects from the tomb to their exact scale, matched with material and colour. This allows visitors to get close to objects, the majority of which can be displayed without glass.

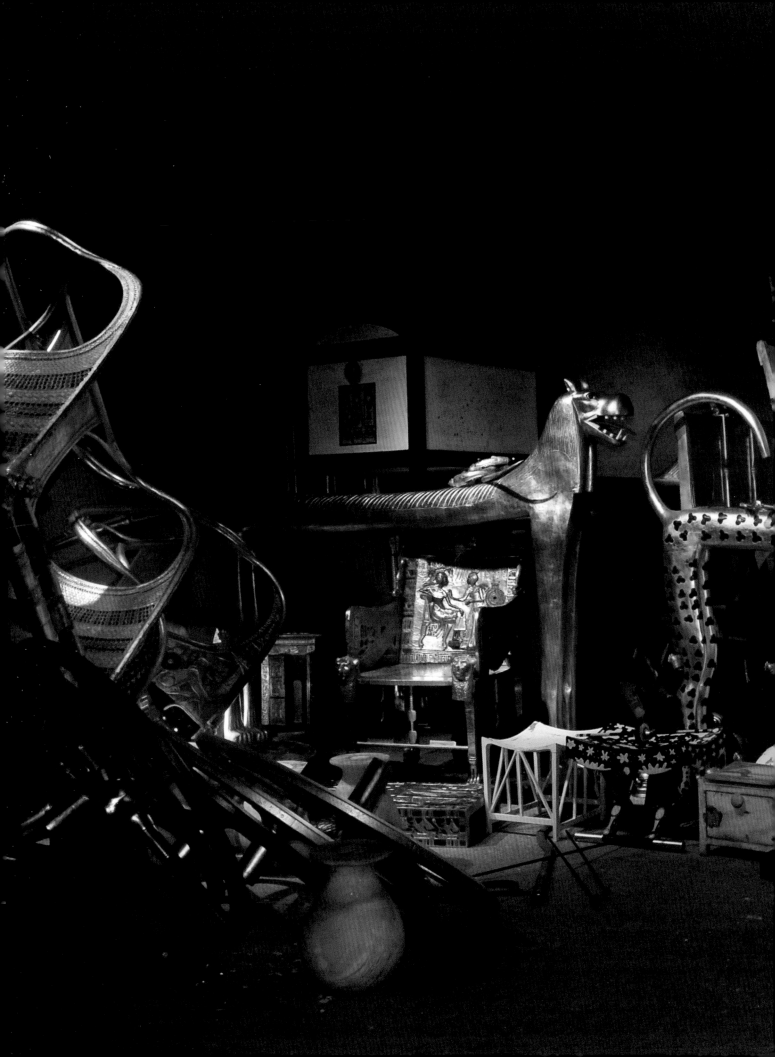

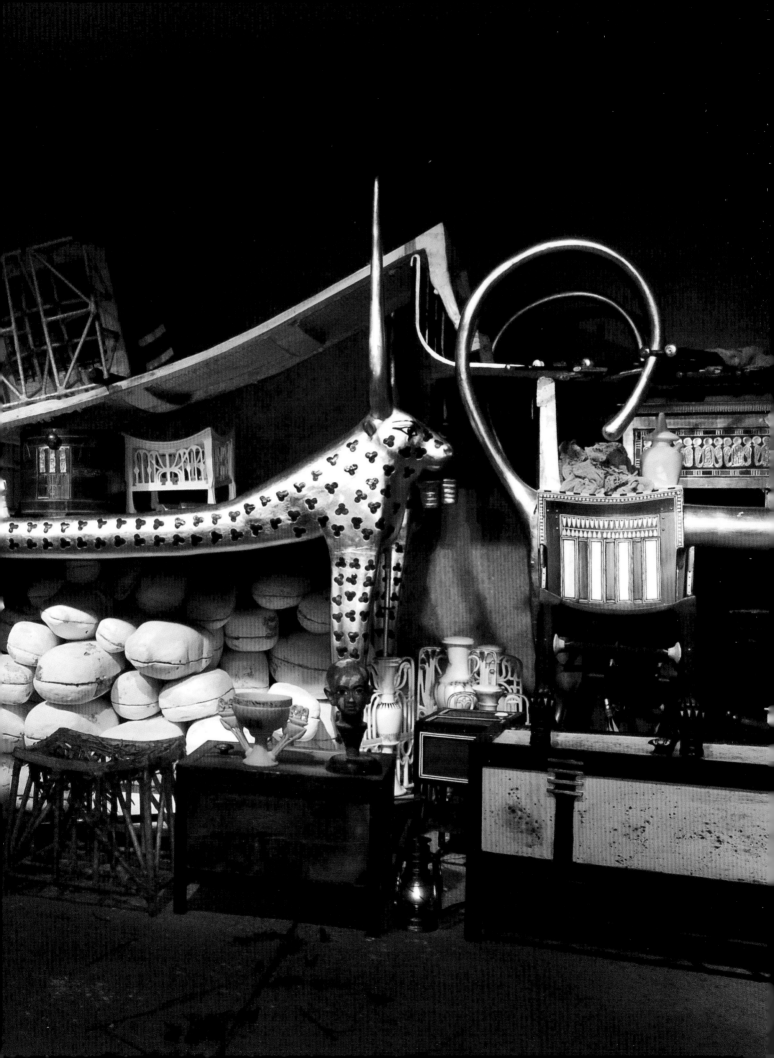

Semmel Concert's replicas of objects from the tomb used to reconstruct the Antechamber.

Photographs by Harry Burton of statues wrapped in linen as first discovered.

Researching the Tomb and its Contents

Statues Unwrapped

Burton's photographs not only allow us to understand the context of objects in the tomb; they also give an extraordinary insight into ancient Egyptian rituals. A recurring feature of many of the figures in the tomb is that they were wrapped in linen cloth. This was an important part of concealing and dressing the objects to make them magically effective.

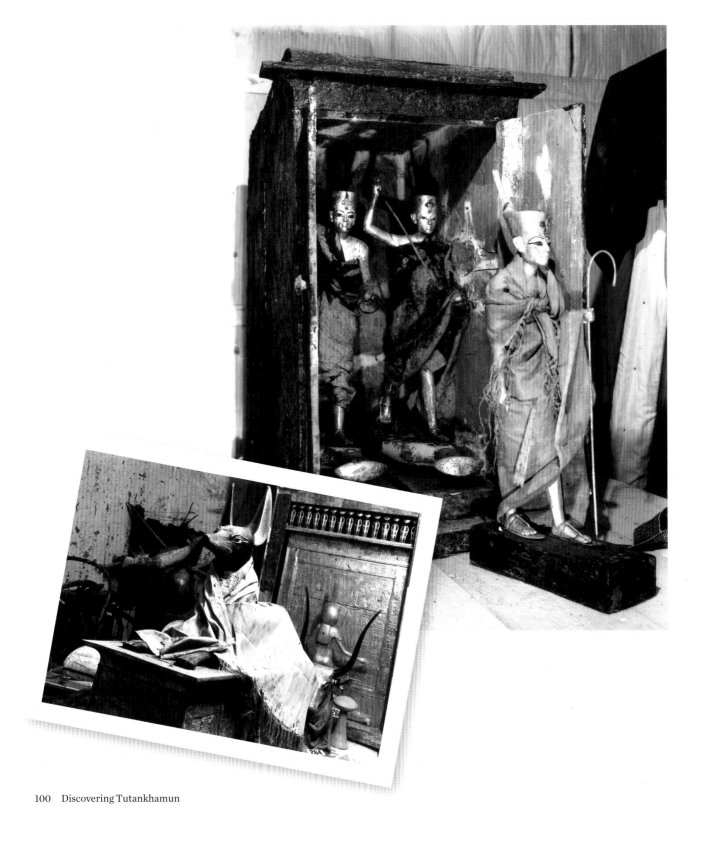

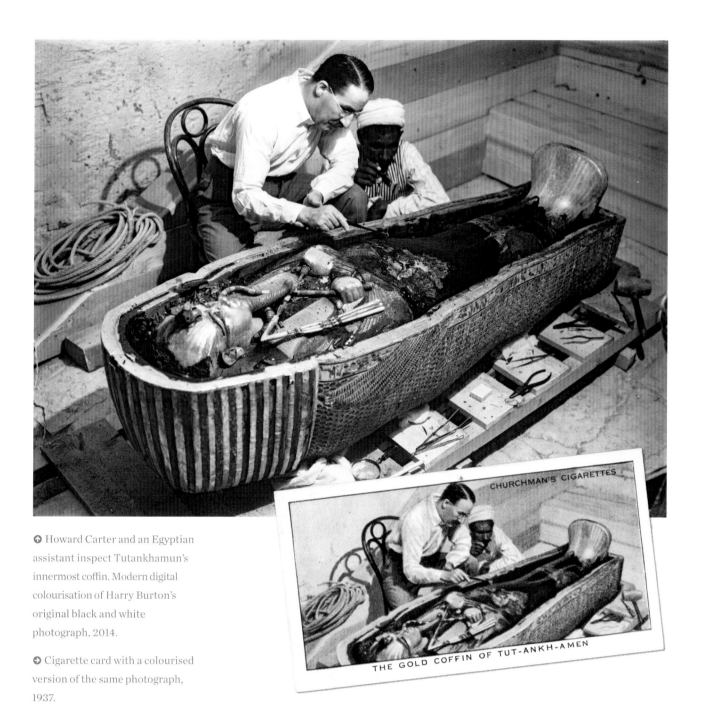

CHURCHMAN'S CIGARETTES

THE GOLD COFFIN OF TUT-ANKH-AMEN

⬆ Howard Carter and an Egyptian assistant inspect Tutankhamun's innermost coffin. Modern digital colourisation of Harry Burton's original black and white photograph, 2014.

➡ Cigarette card with a colourised version of the same photograph, 1937.

Colourisation

Carter was at pains to highlight the colour of objects in Tutankhamun's tomb. In the absence of successful colour photography, he resorted to annotating black and white prints and record cards of individual objects with detailed descriptions of the materials used and the colours observed. Attempts at colourising Burton's photographs were made in the decades following the discovery of the tomb, but modern computer technology dramatically improves on these attempts. The image above, and on pp's 30–31 were produced for this publication drawing on information contained in the Carter Archive, as well as modern photographs of the objects in the Egyptian Museum, Cairo.

Technical Studies

The true value of the objects in Tutankhamun's tomb lies in their potential to provide an unrivalled understanding of ancient Egyptian art, technology and manufacture in the middle of the second millennium BC. A look at the books listed below – all published by the Griffith Institute – reveals the limited range of objects that have been researched. With only 30 per cent of the contents of the tomb studied to date, there remains much to discover.

Baines, J (ed), 1994. *Stone vessels, pottery, and sealings from the tomb of Tutankhamun* by Ali A R H el-Khouli, R Holthoer, C A Hope and O E Kaper.

Beinlich, H and M Saleh, 1989. *Corpus der hieroglyphischen Inschriften aus dem Grab des Tutanchamun.*

Černý, J, 1965. *Hieratic inscriptions from the tomb of Tutankhamun.*

Davies, N M and A H Gardiner, 1962. *Tutankhamun's painted box.*

Eaton-Krauss, M and E Graefe, 1985. *The small golden shrine from the tomb of Tutankhamun.*

Eaton-Krauss, M, 1993. *The sarcophagus in the tomb of Tutankhamun.*

Eaton-Krauss, M, 2008. *The thrones, chairs, stools, and footstools from the tomb of Tutankhamun.*

Filce Leek, F, 1972. *The human remains from the tomb of Tutankhamun.*

Jones, D, 1990. *Model boats from the tomb of Tutankhamun.*

Littauer M A and J H Crouwel, 1985. *Chariots and related equipment from the tomb of Tutankhamun.*

Manniche, L, 1976. *Musical instruments from the tomb of Tutankhamun.*

McLeod, W, 1970. *Composite bows from the tomb of Tutankhamun.*

McLeod, W, 1982. *Self bows and other archery tackle from the tomb of Tutankhamun.*

Murray, H and M Nuttall, 1963. *A handlist to Howard Carter's catalogue of objects in Tutankhamun's tomb.*

Tait, W J, 1982. *Game boxes and accessories from the tomb of Tutankhamun.*

'With only 30 per cent of the contents of the tomb studied to date, there remains much to discover.'

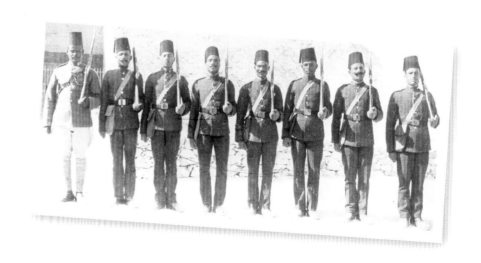

◗ A group of Egyptian soldiers on guard duty outside the tomb, 1923.

◗ Arthur Mace (left) and Alfred Lucas treat one of the 'guardian' statues in the conservation 'laboratory'.